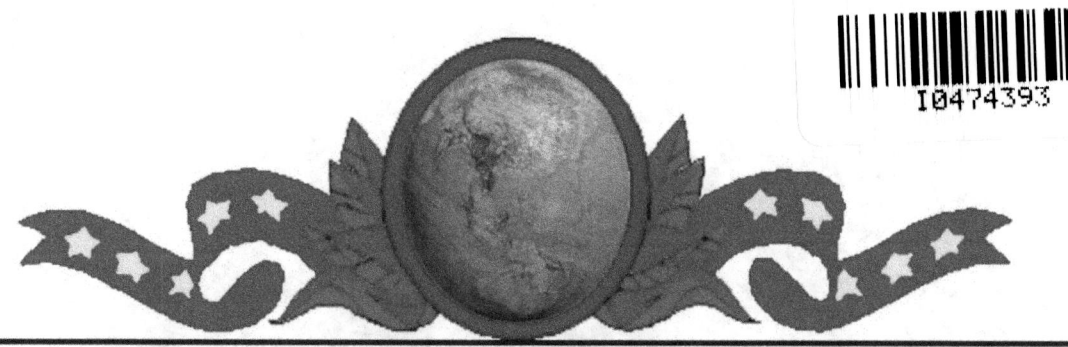

Real World
Colouring Book
For Advanced Users & Adults

Copyright 2019 By John Boom

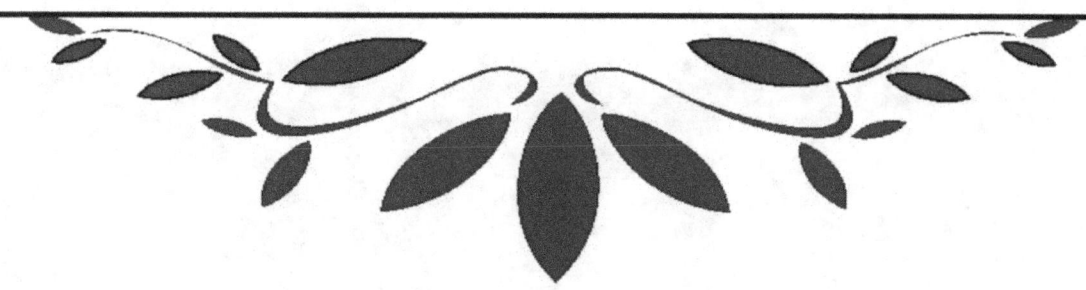

50 Images

Created From Real Life Photos
For You To Colour As You Please.

ISBN 978-0-359-78835-4

9 780359 788354

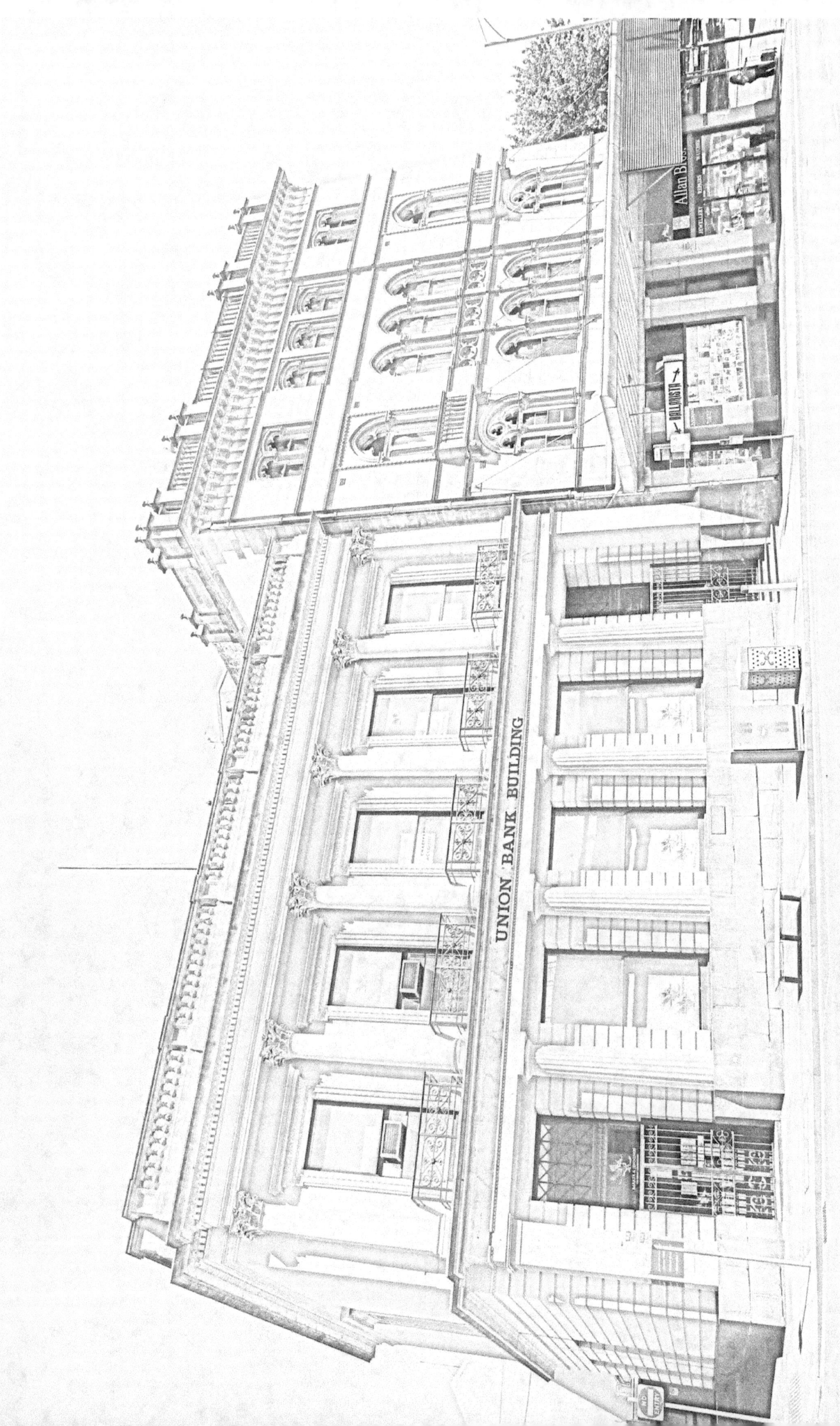

UNION BANK BUILDING

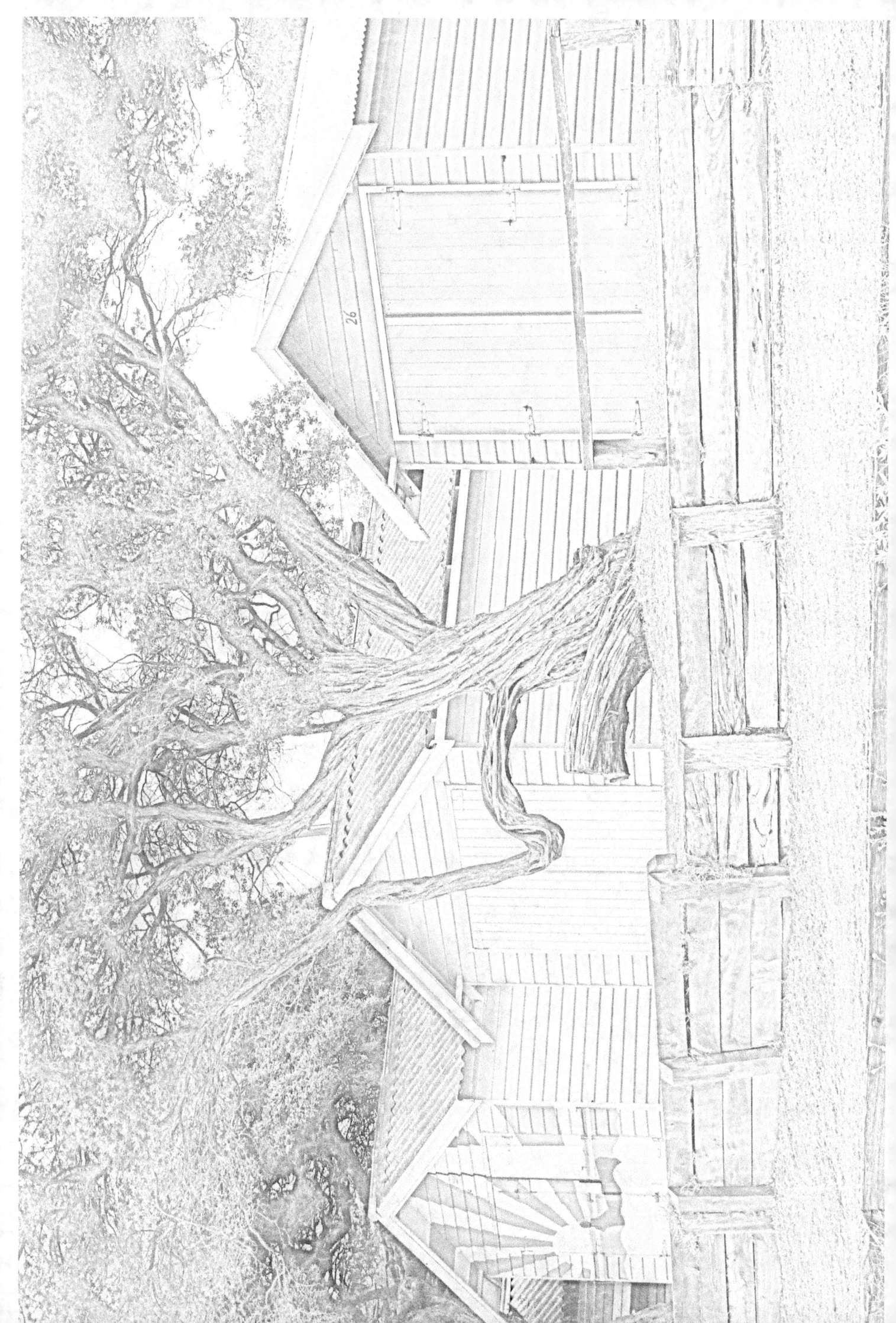

Blue Tongue Lizard

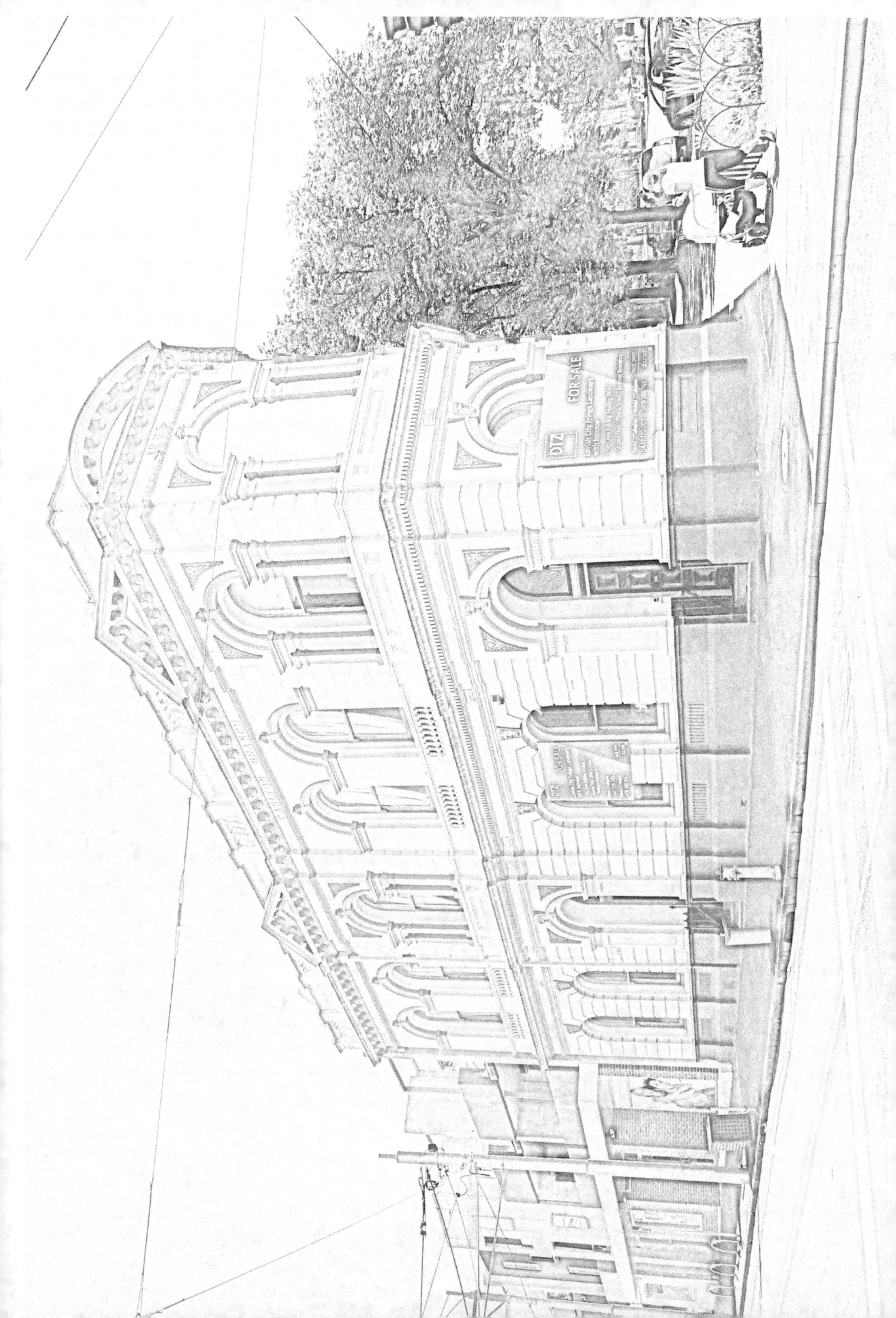

Butterfly

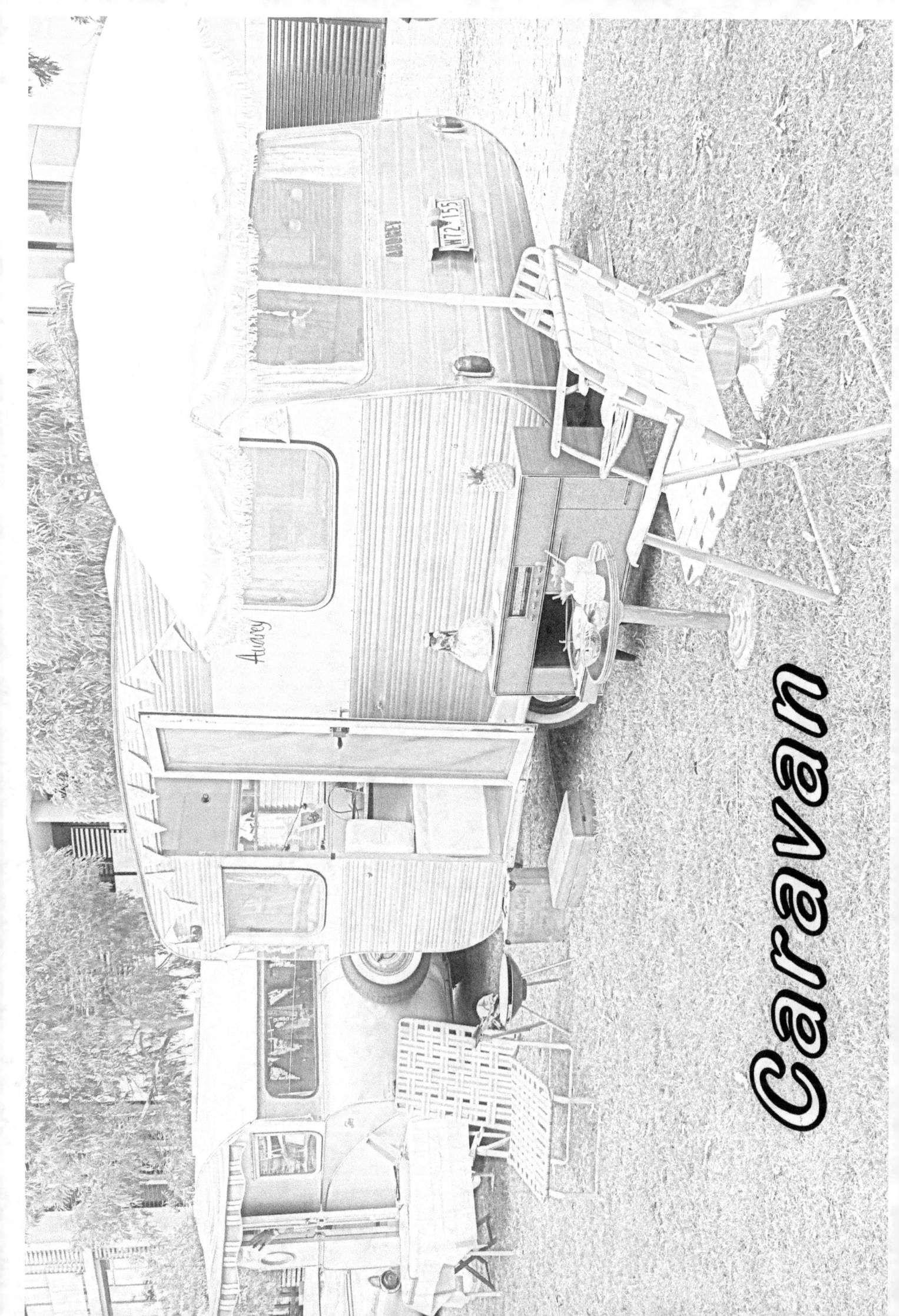

Caravan

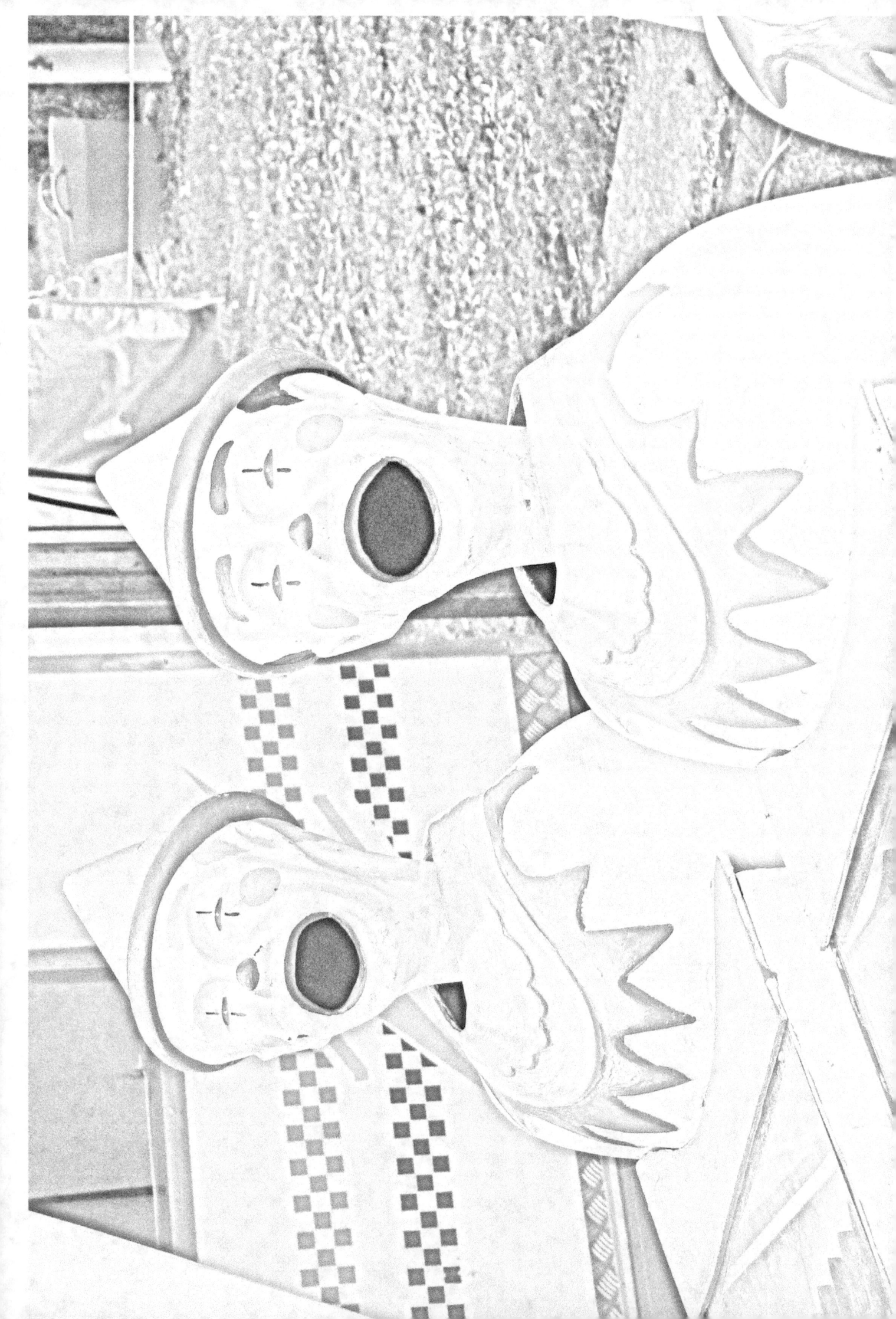

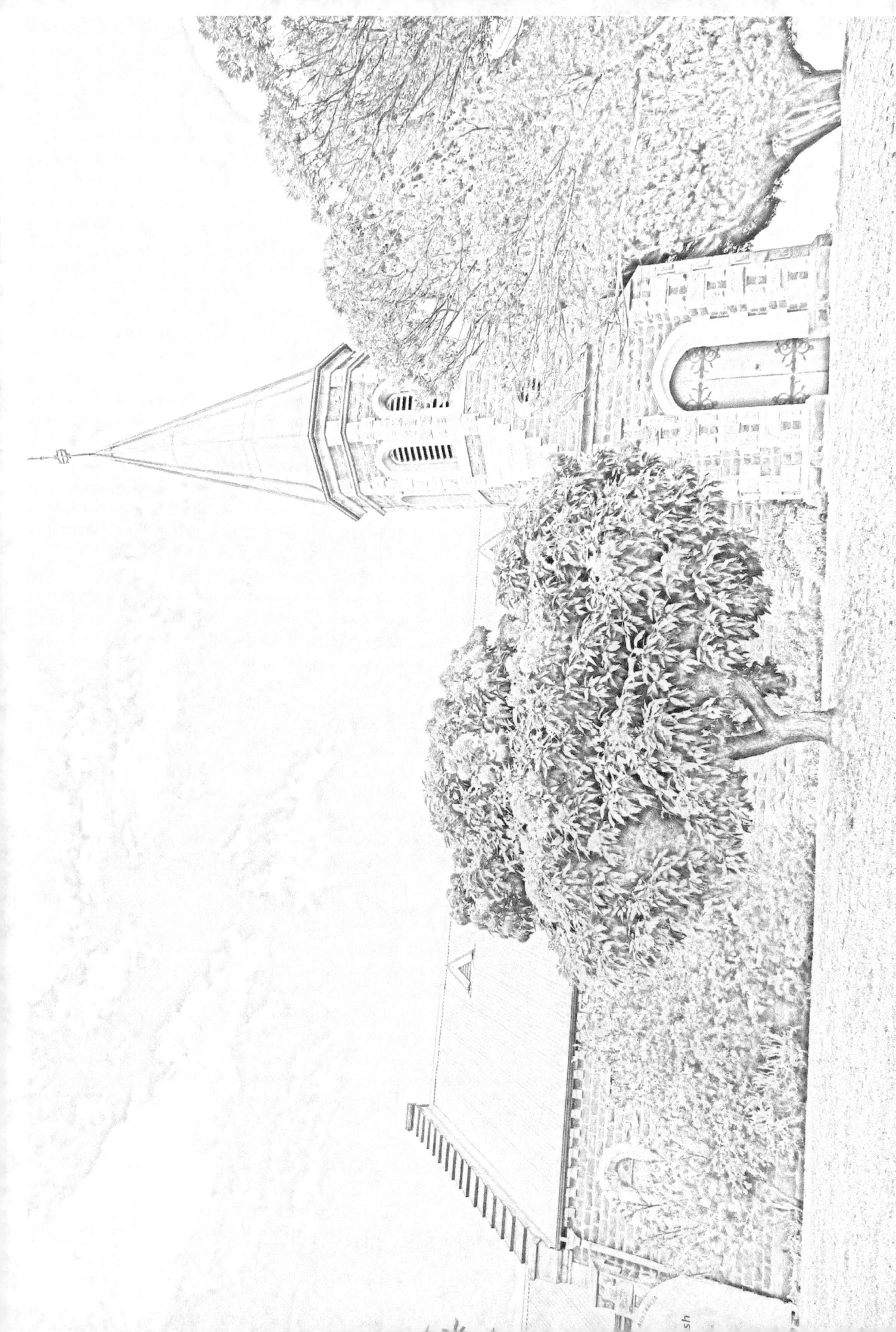

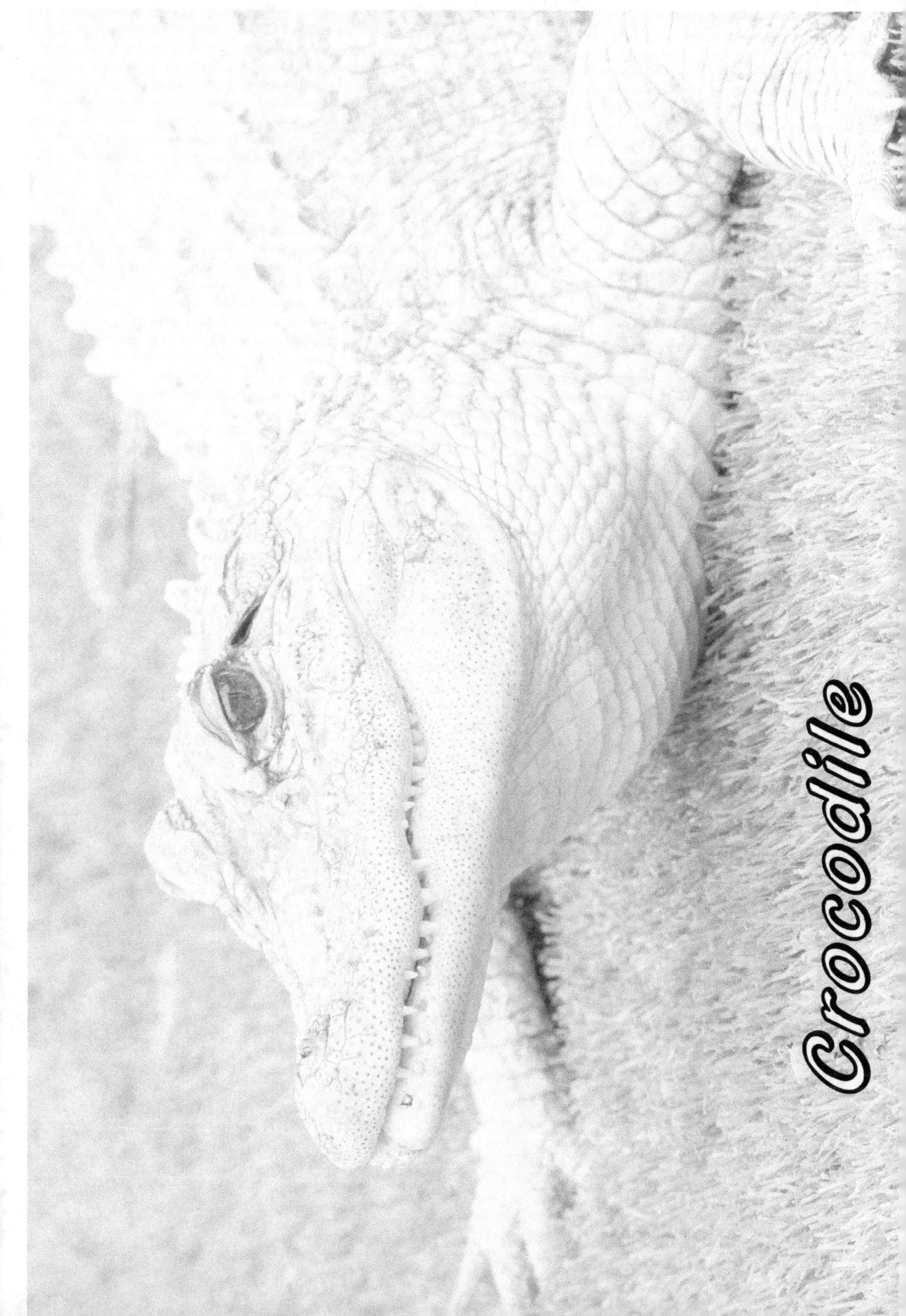

Crocodile

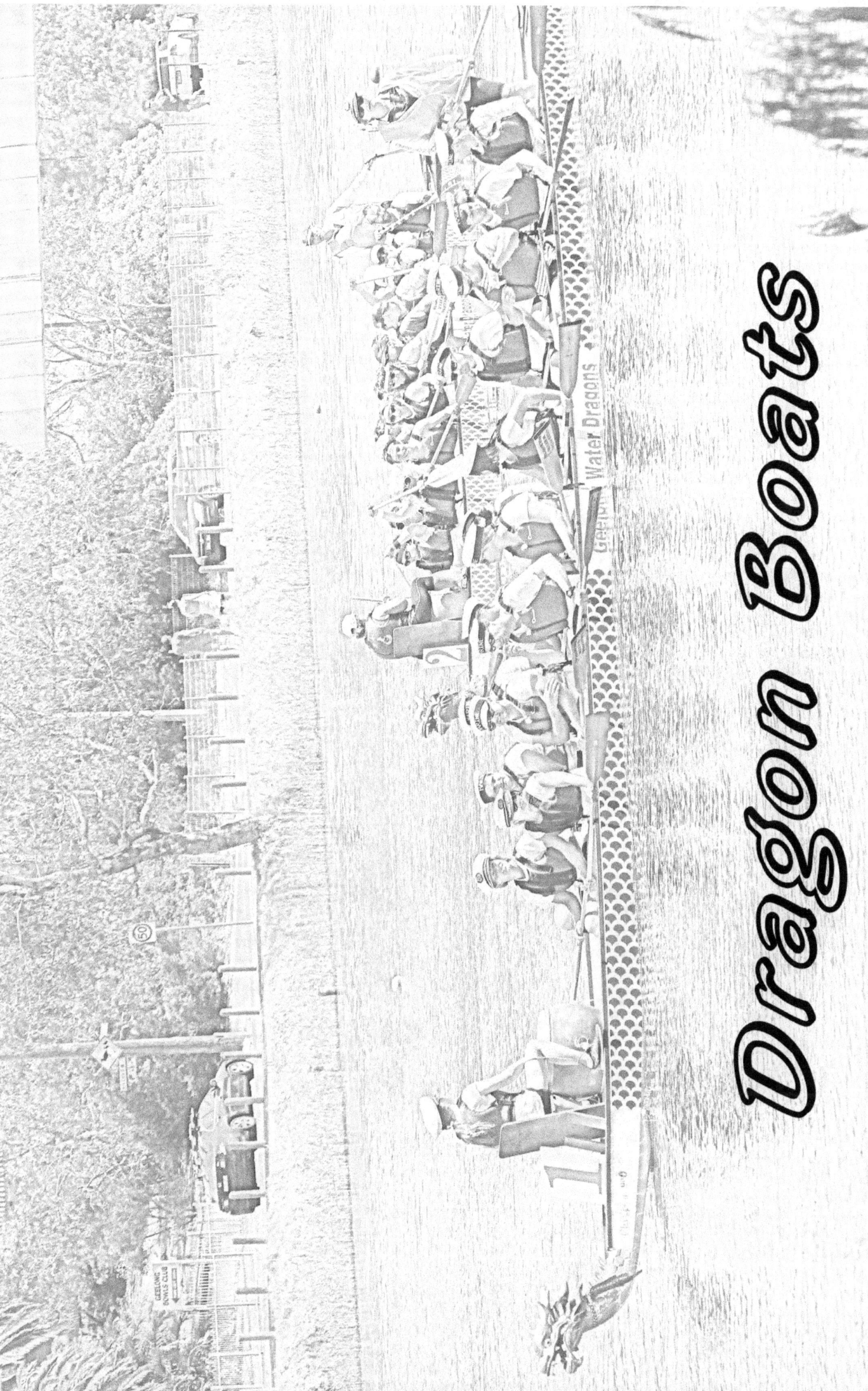

Dragon Boats

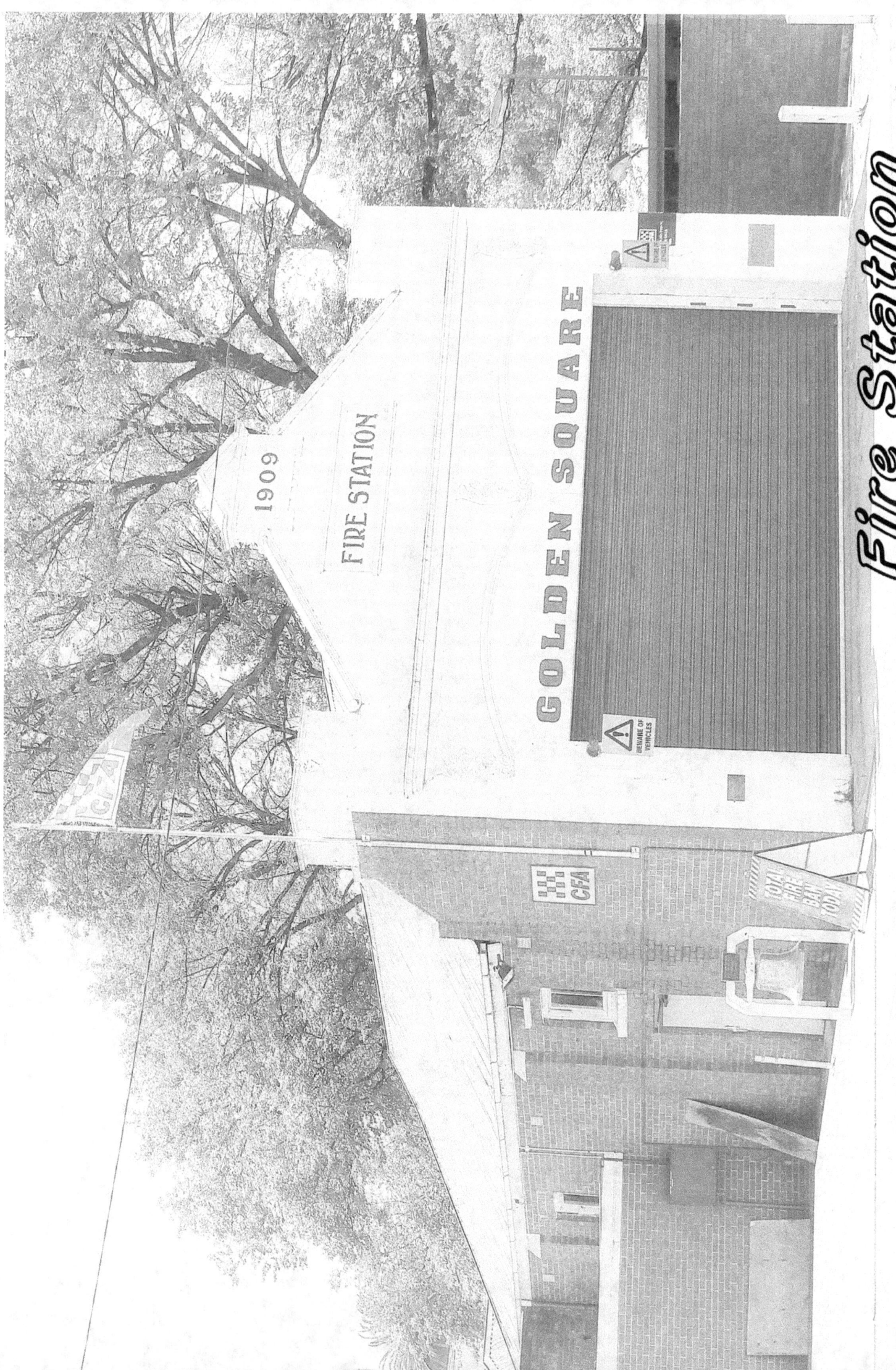

Fire Station

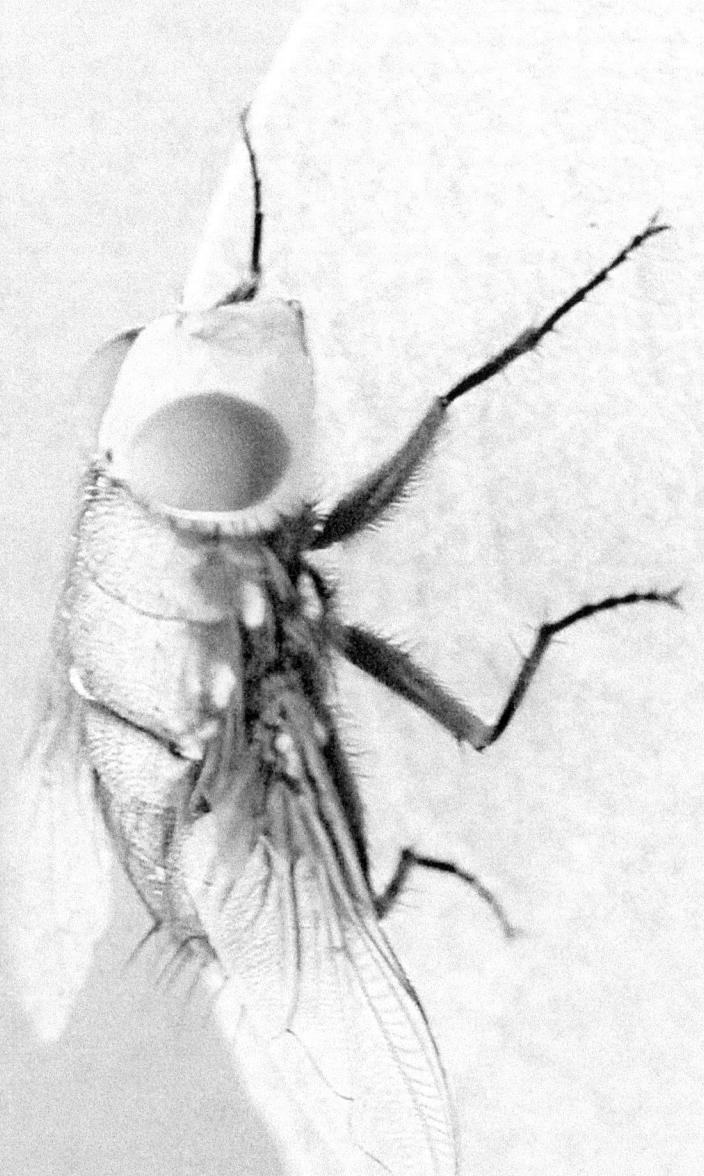

Fly

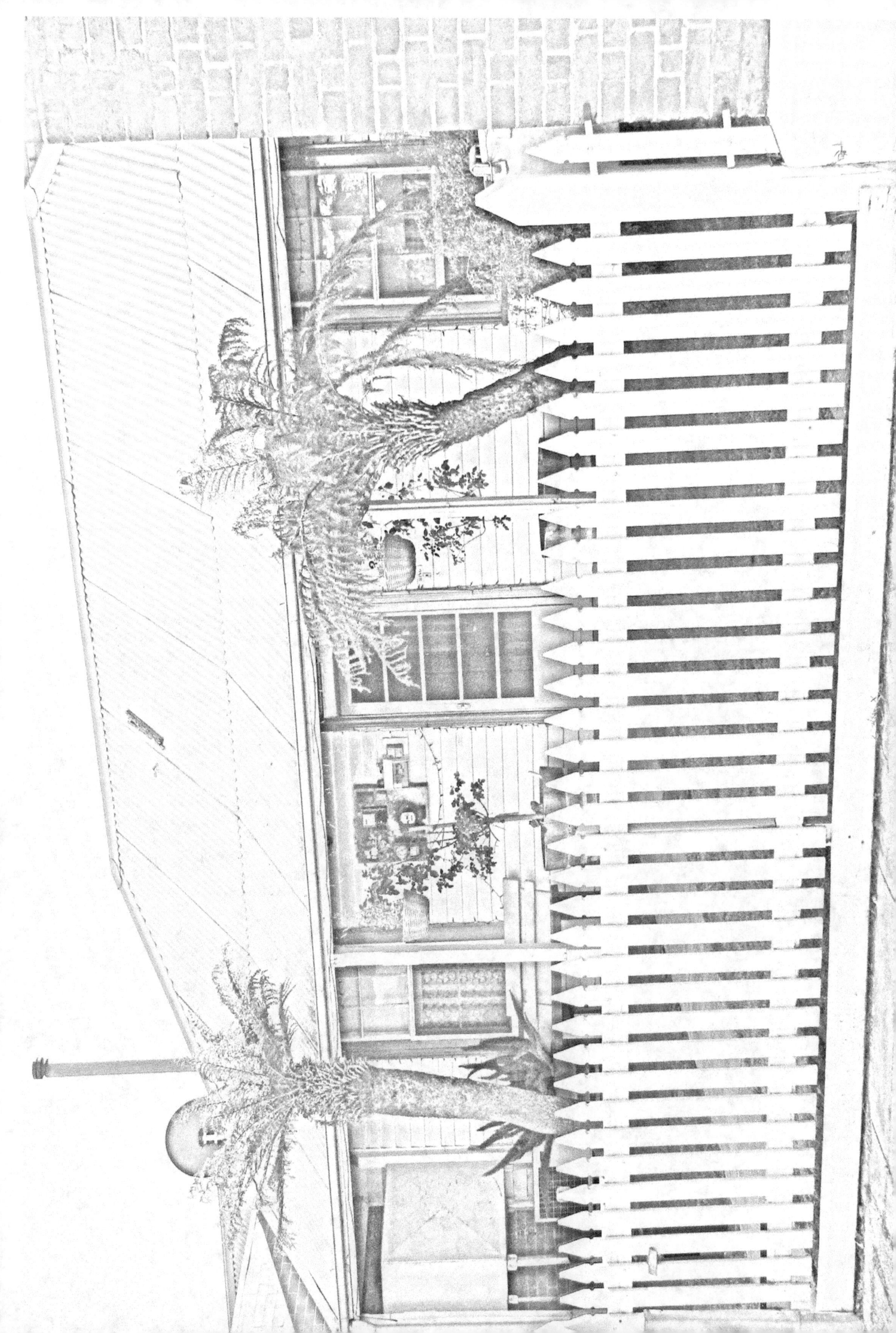

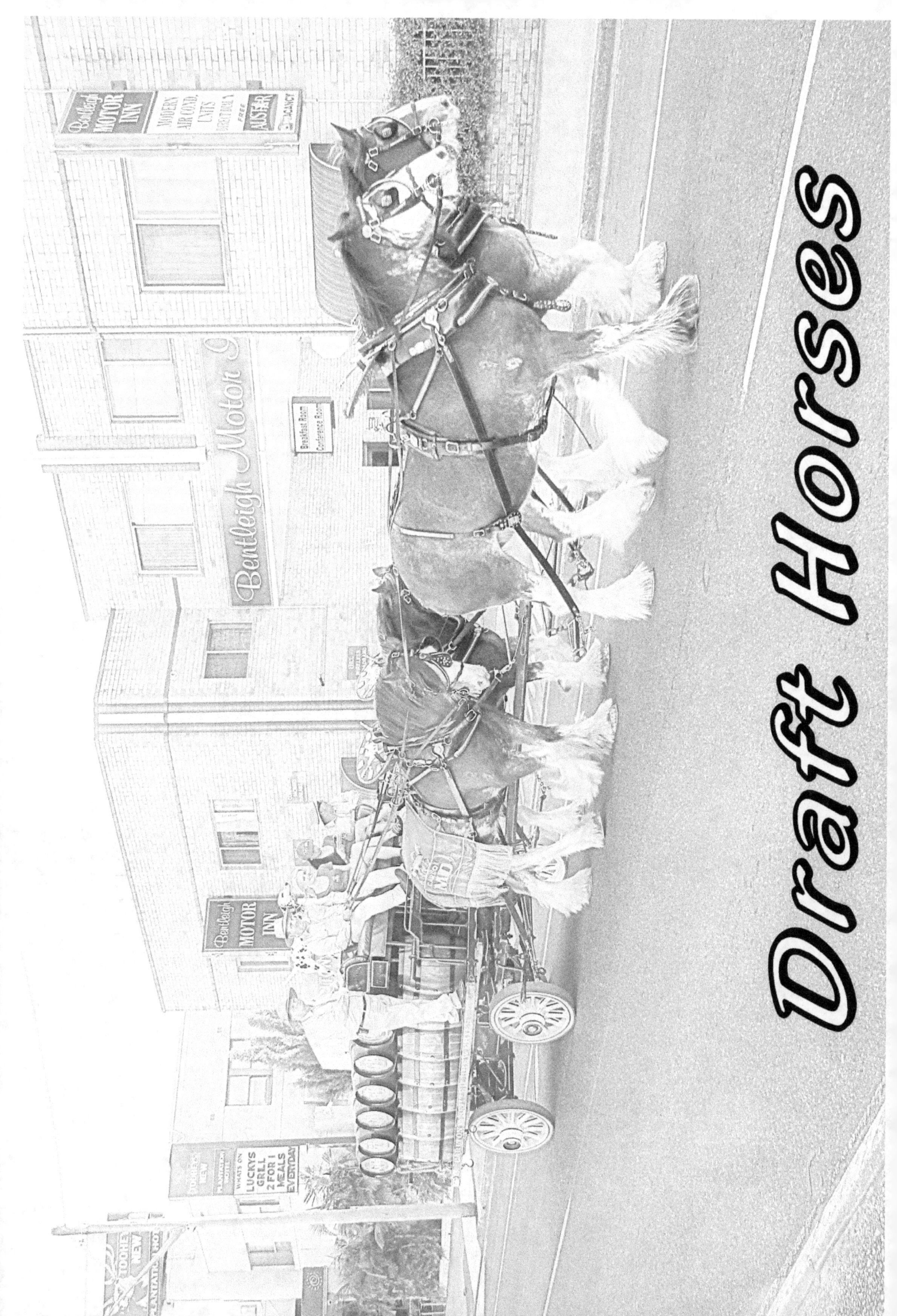

Draft Horses

Hotel

Hotel

WEST COAST HOTEL
EST. 1873

POKIES

Hotel

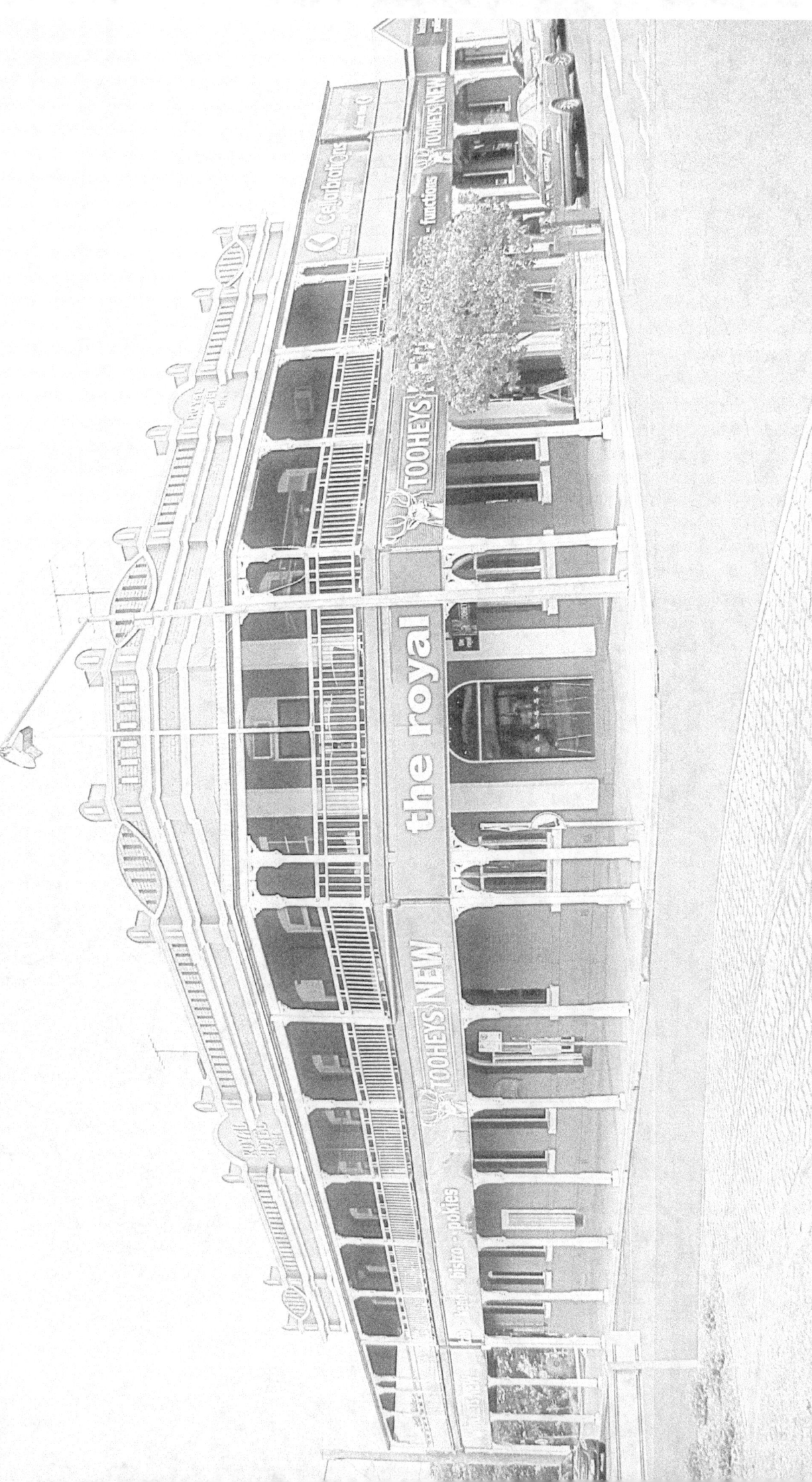

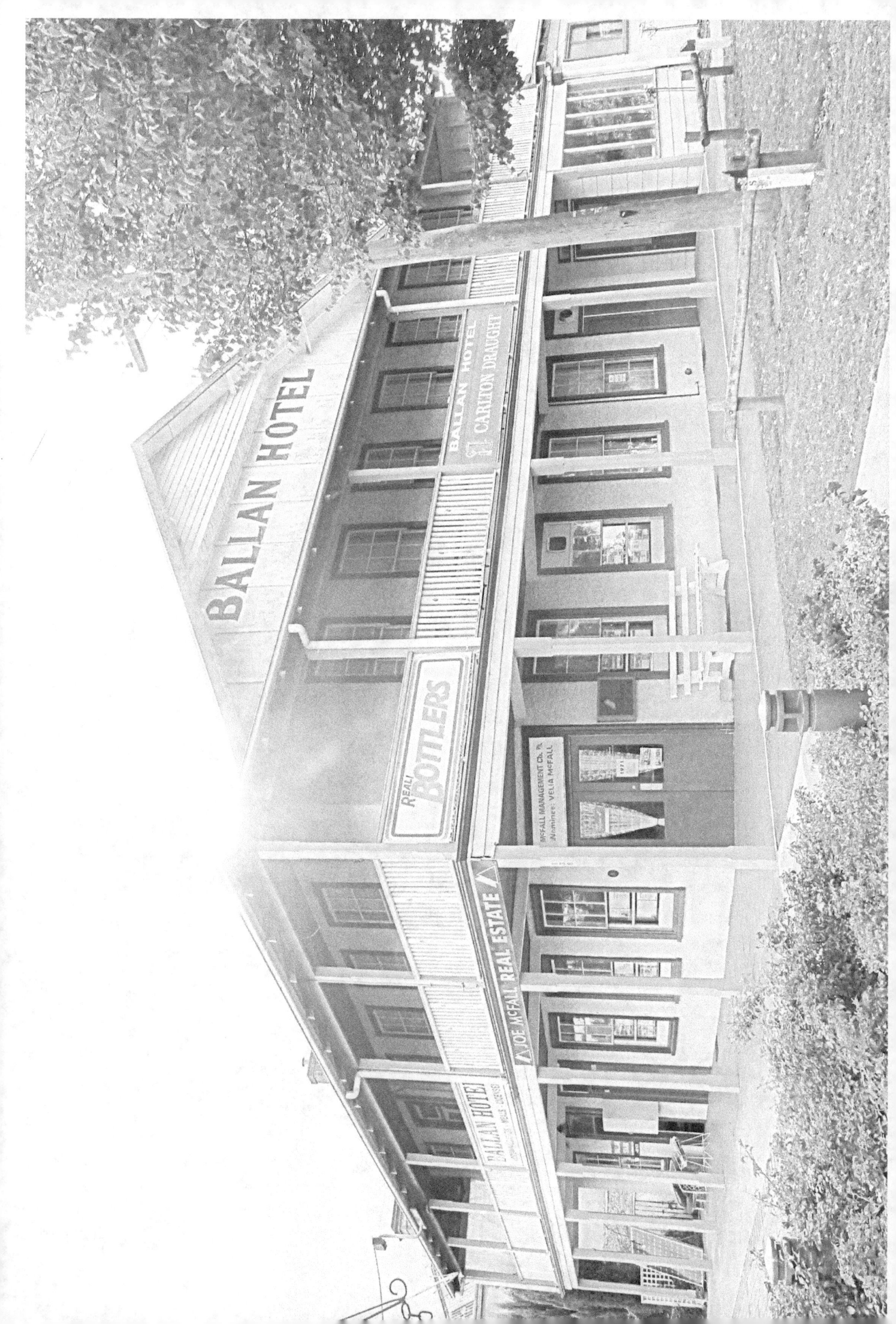

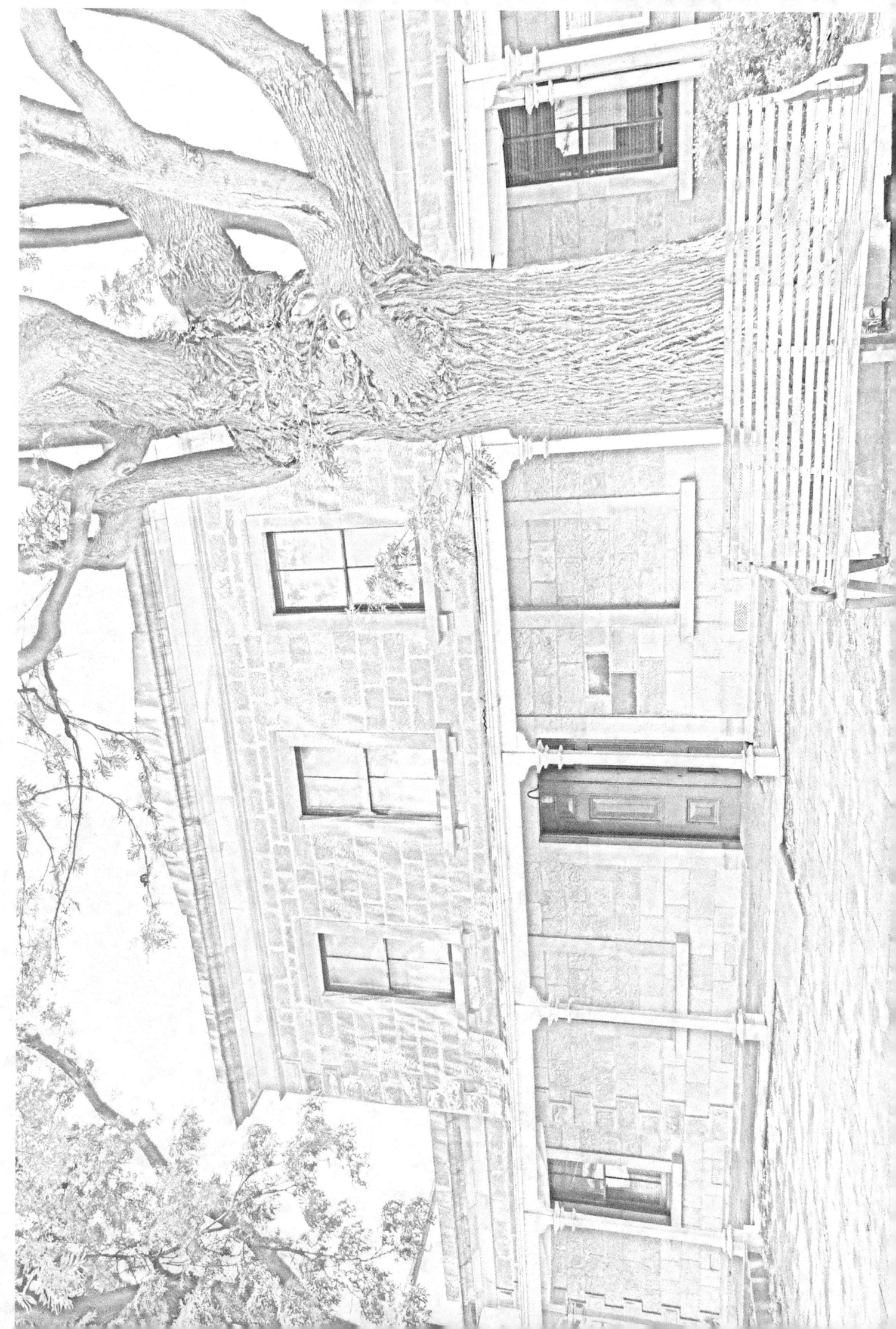

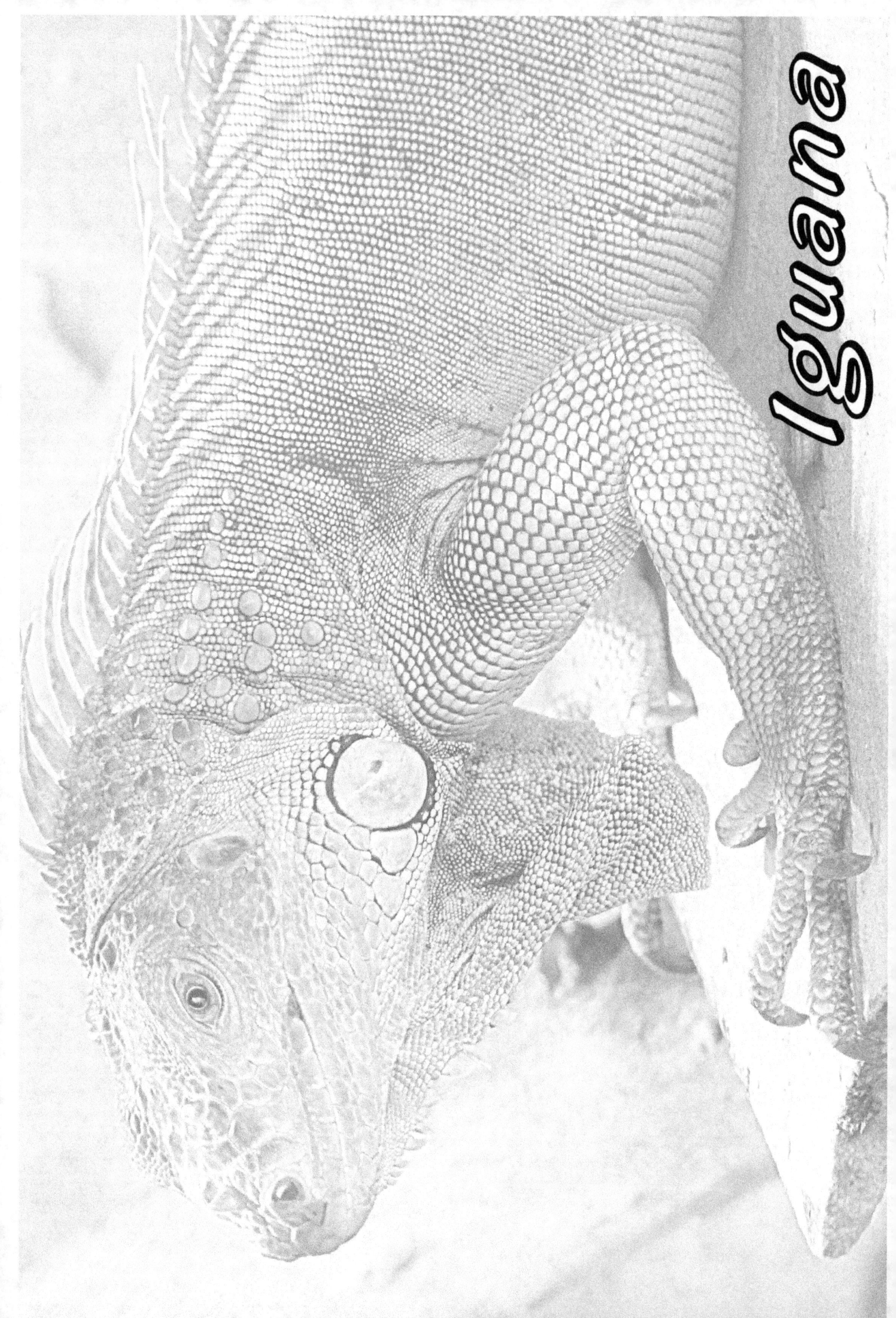

Iguana

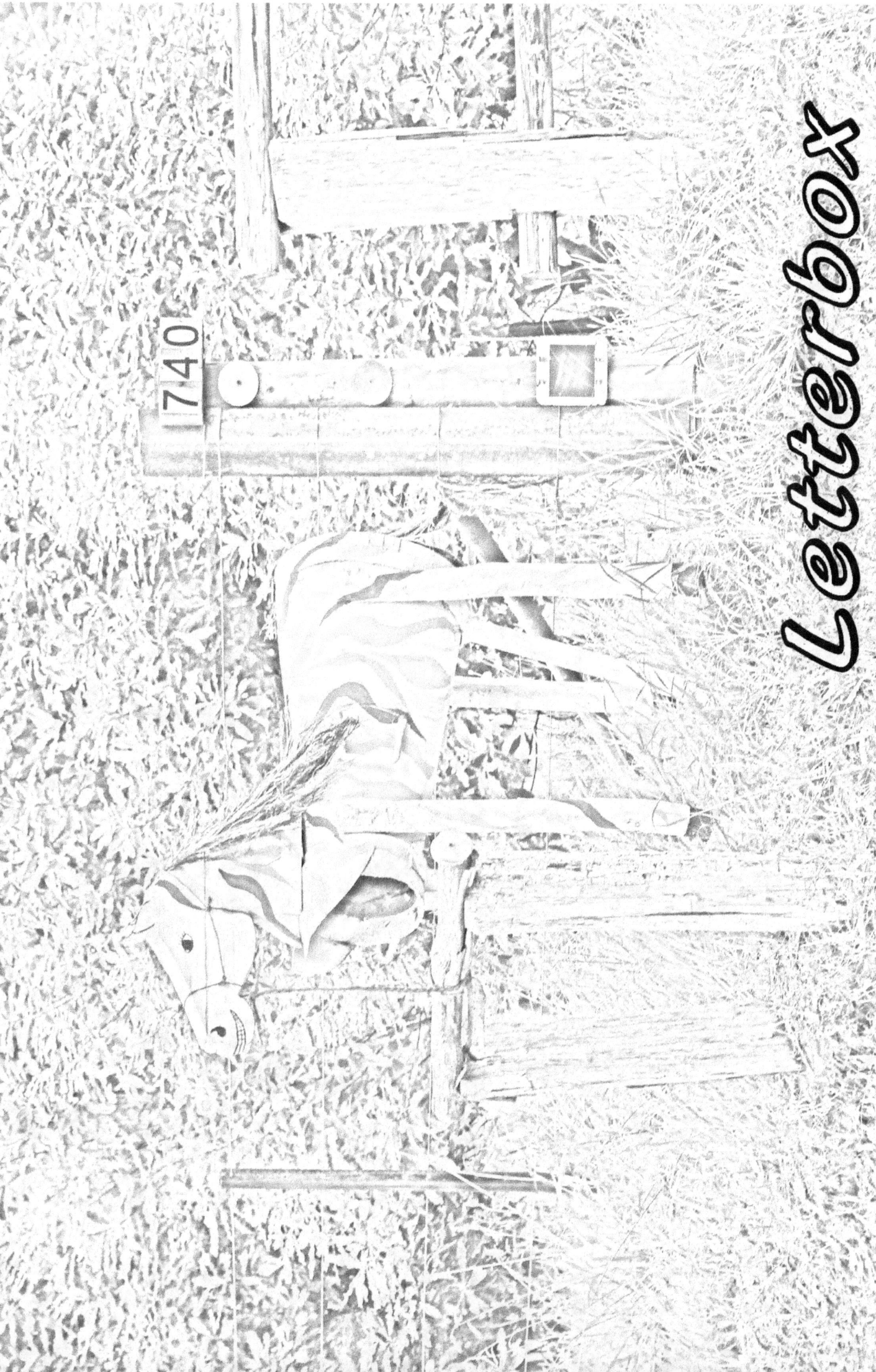

740

Letterbox

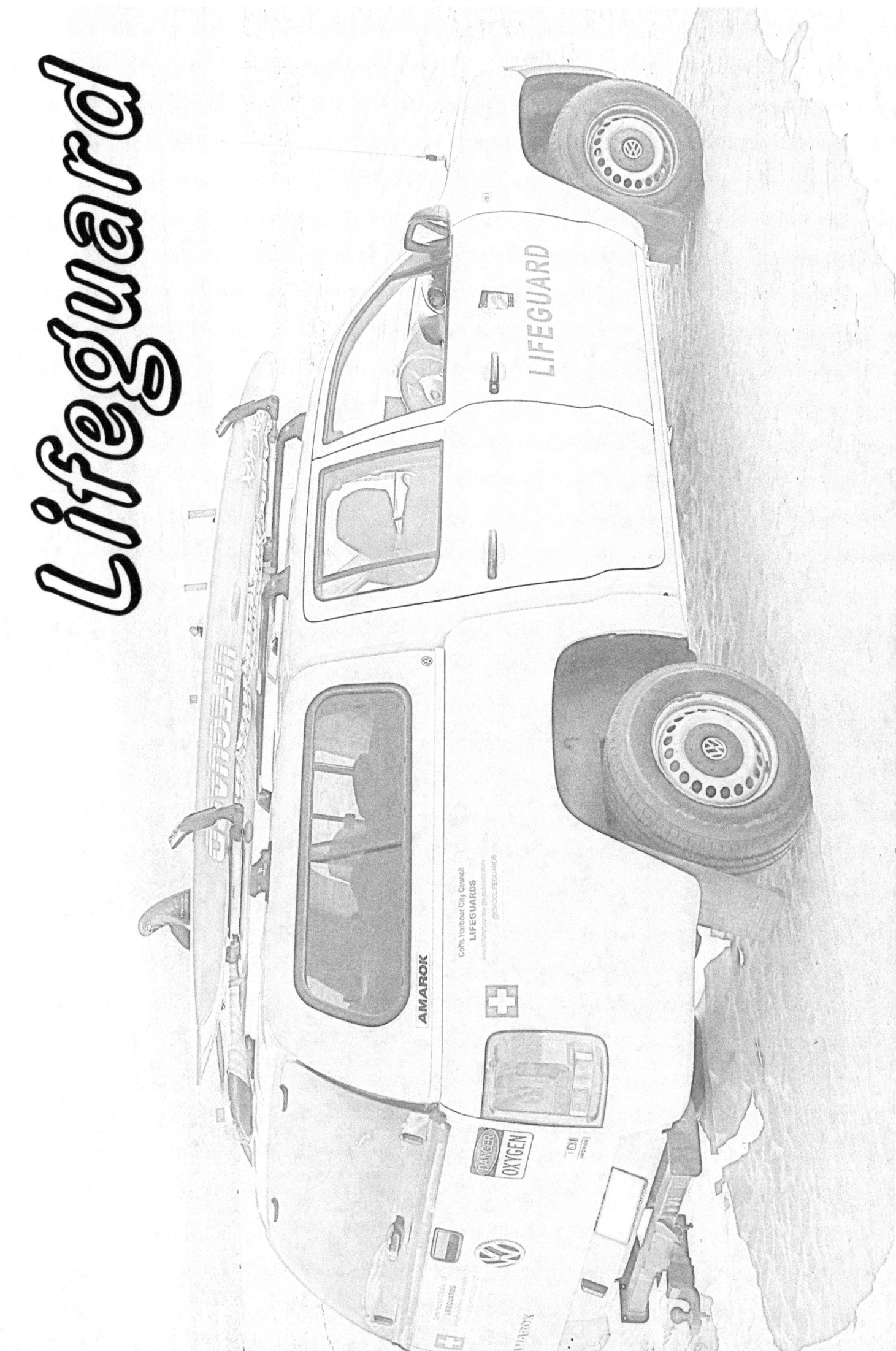

Lifeguard

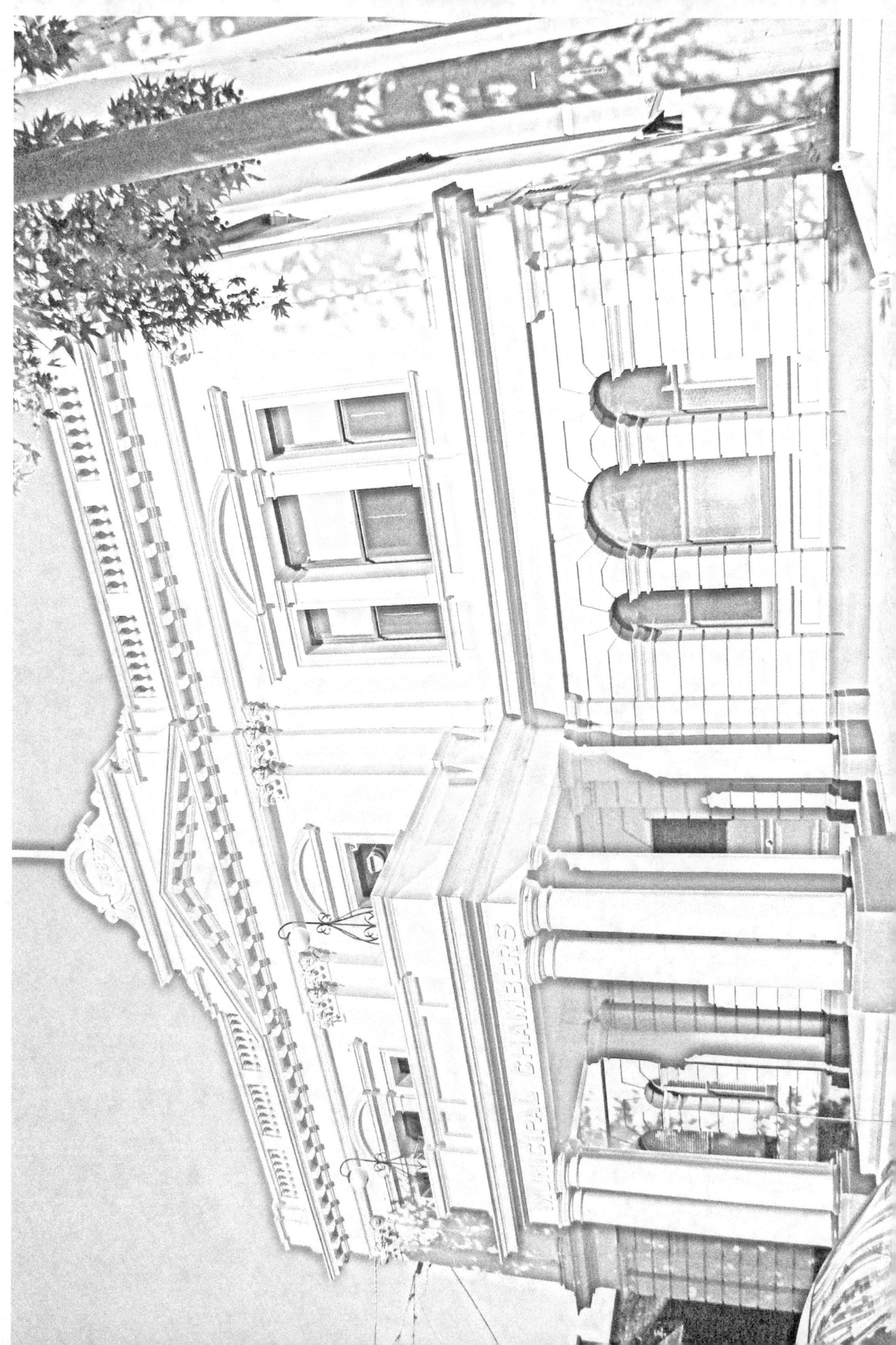

Racing Boat

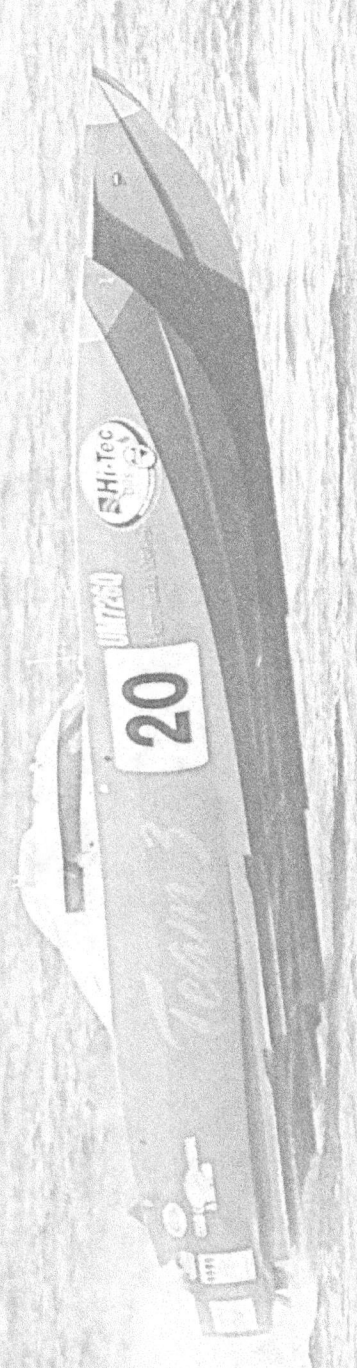

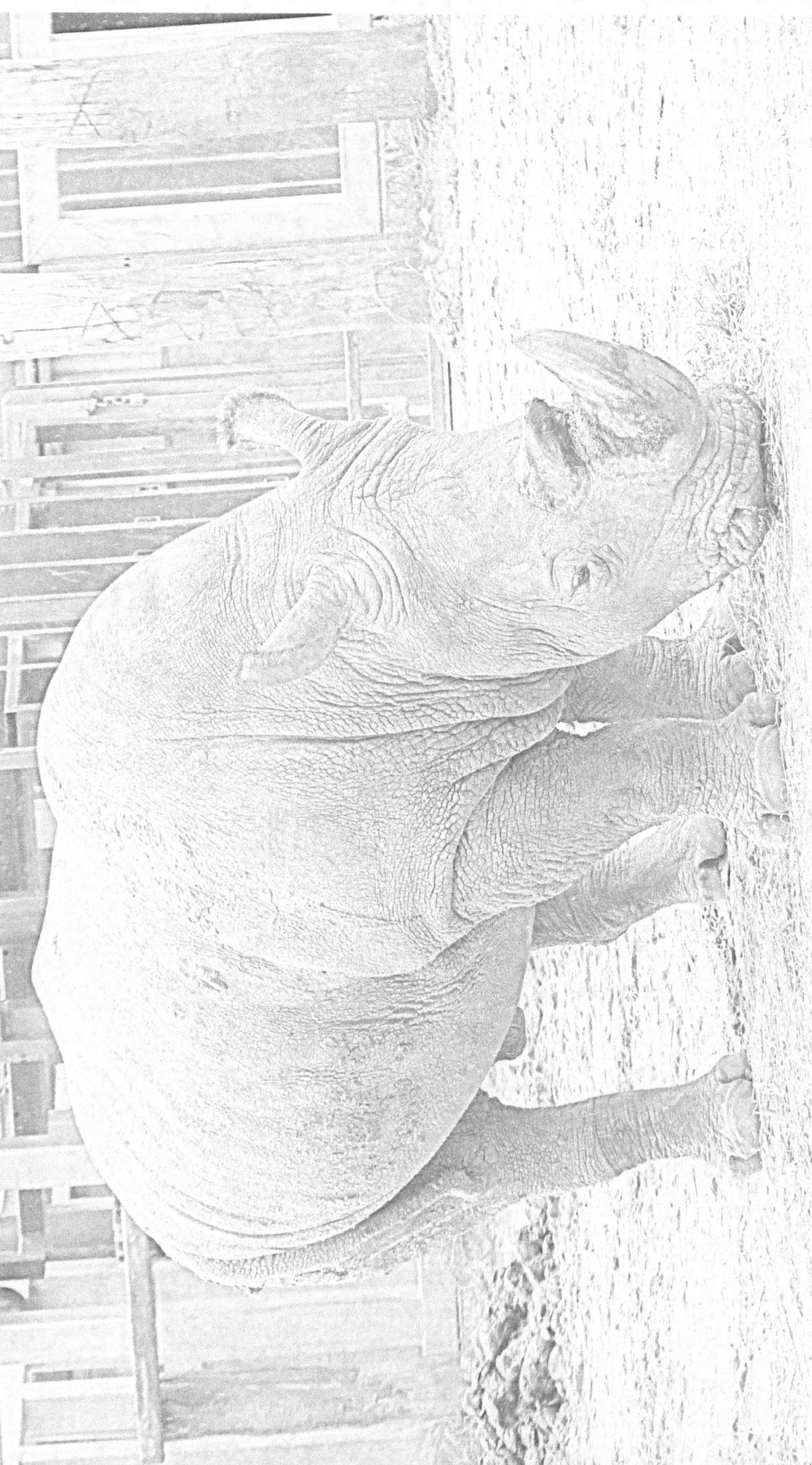

Rhino

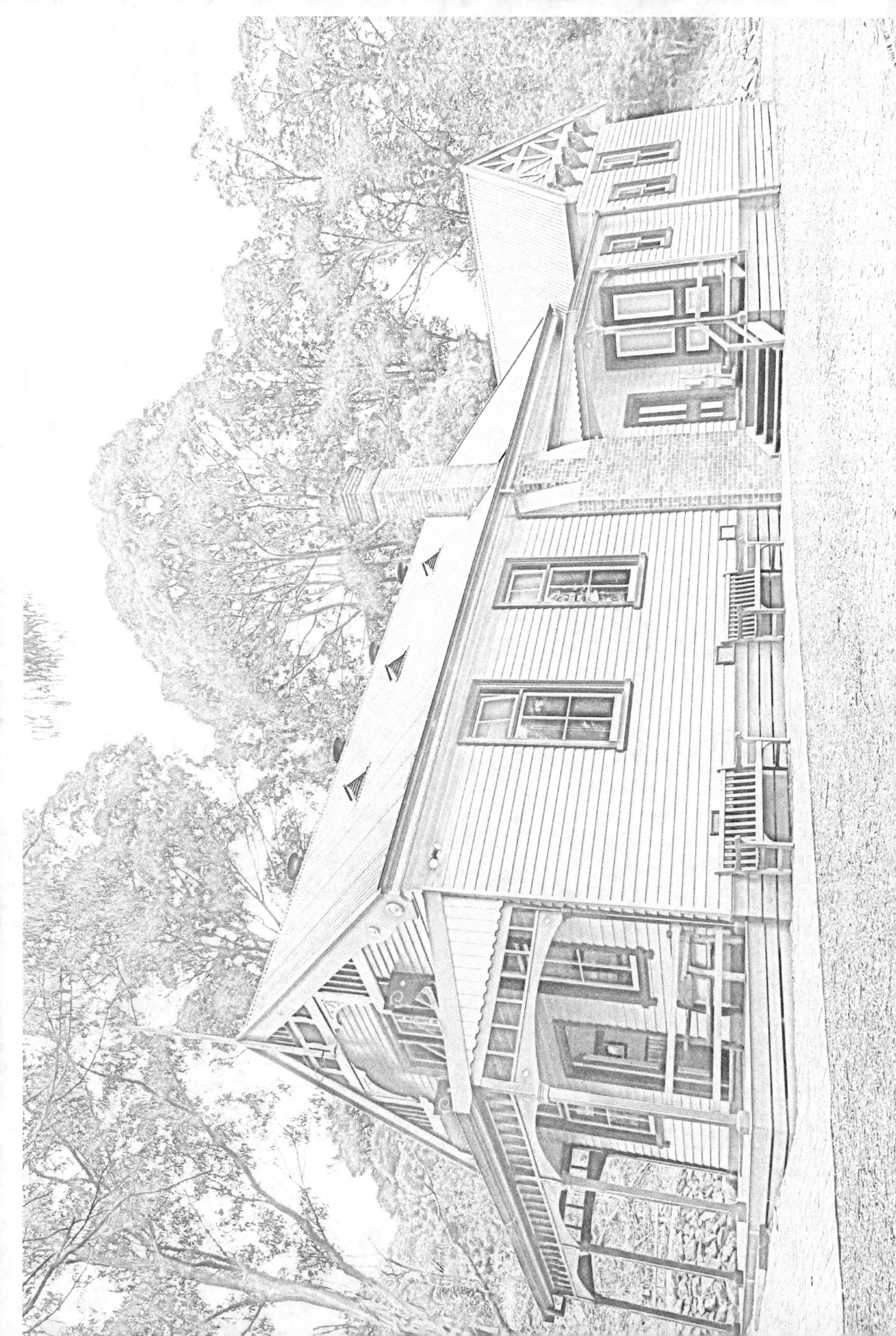

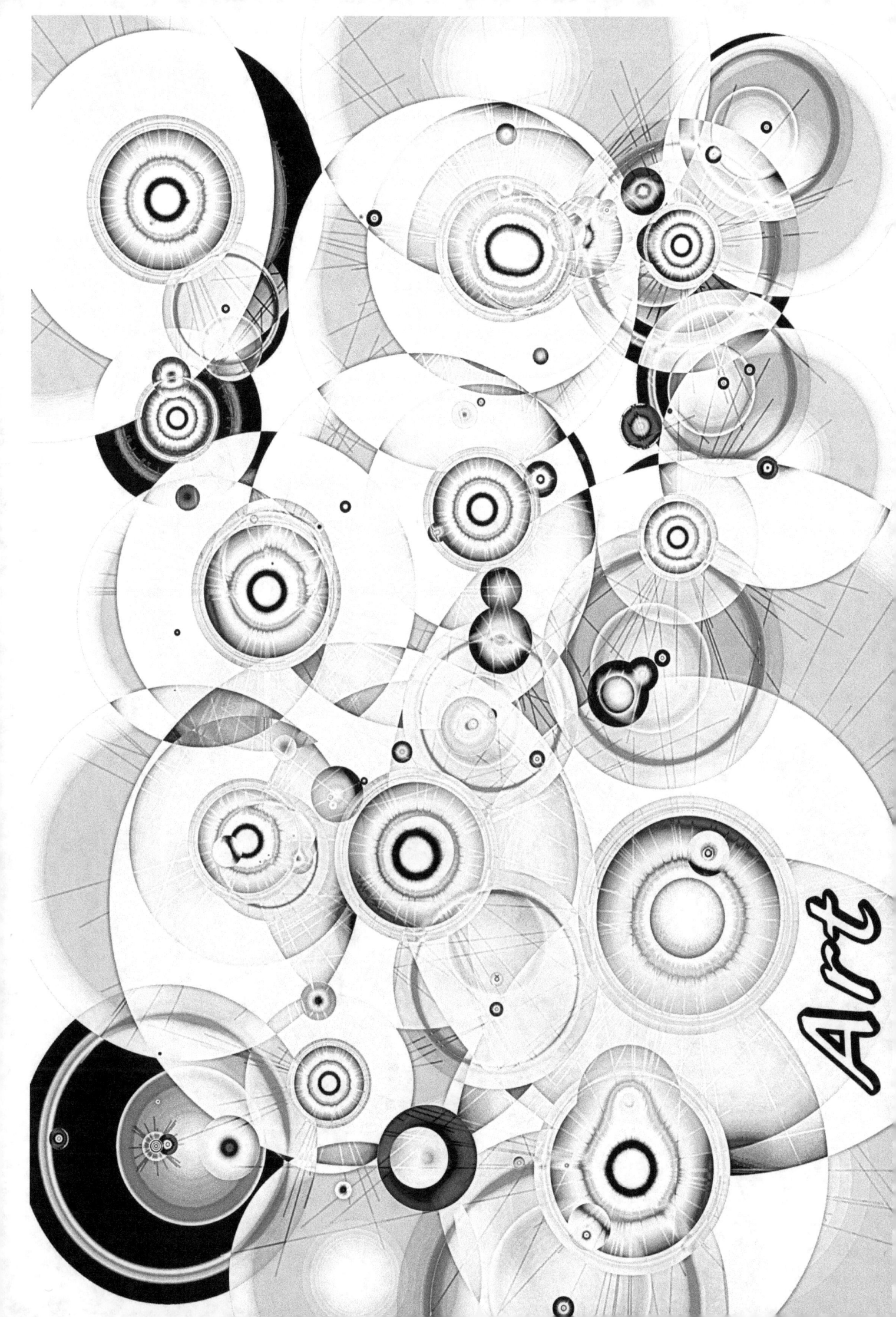

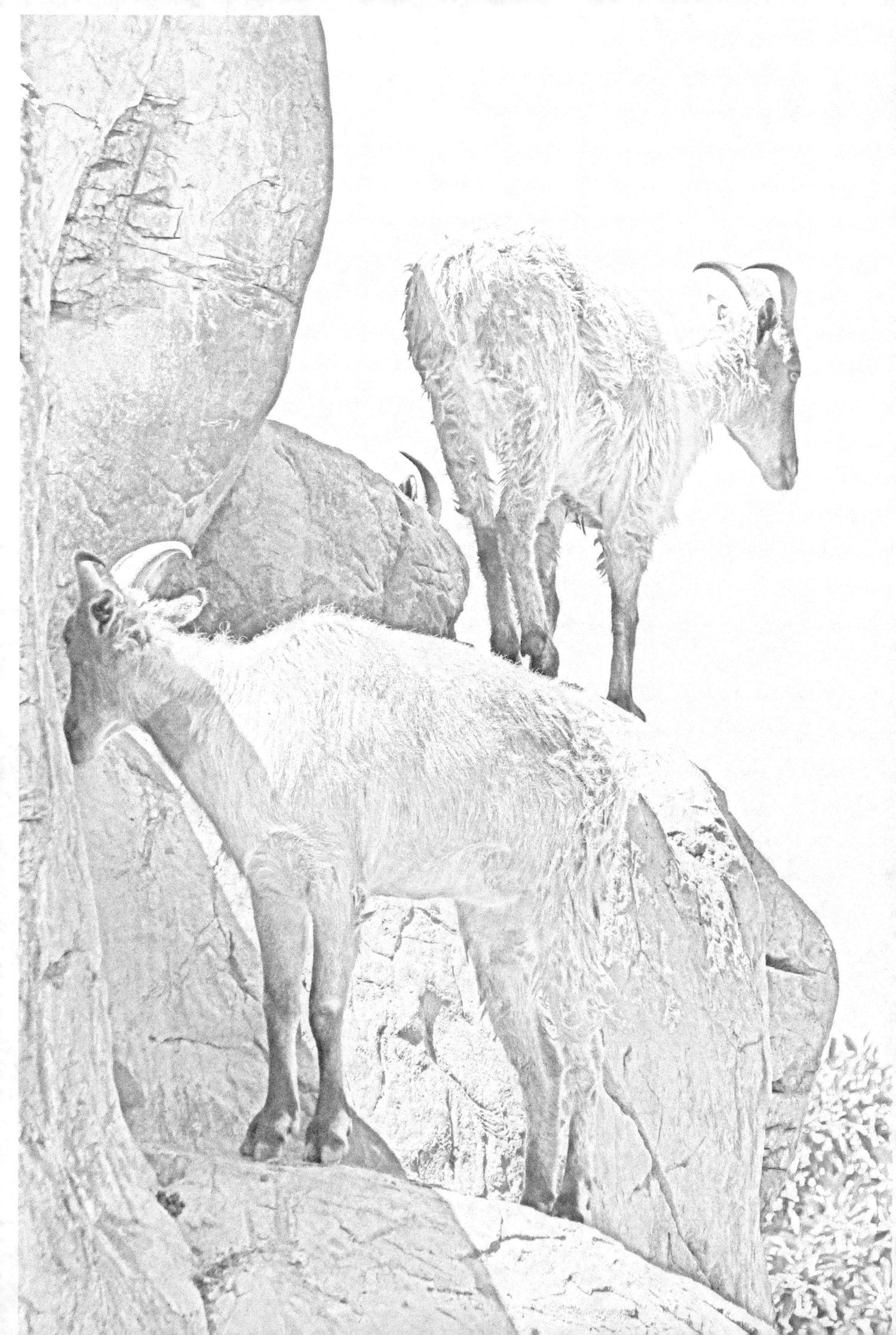

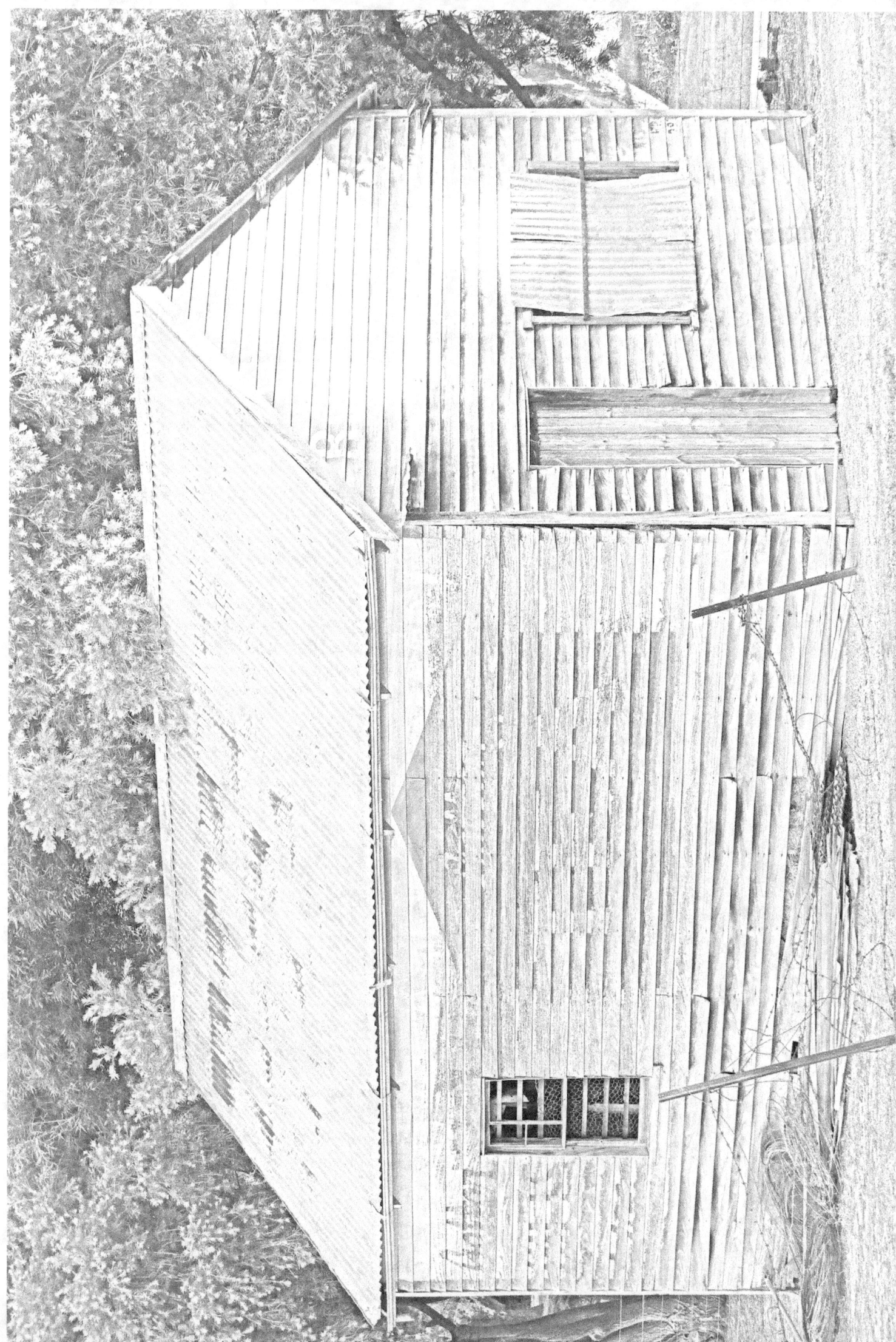

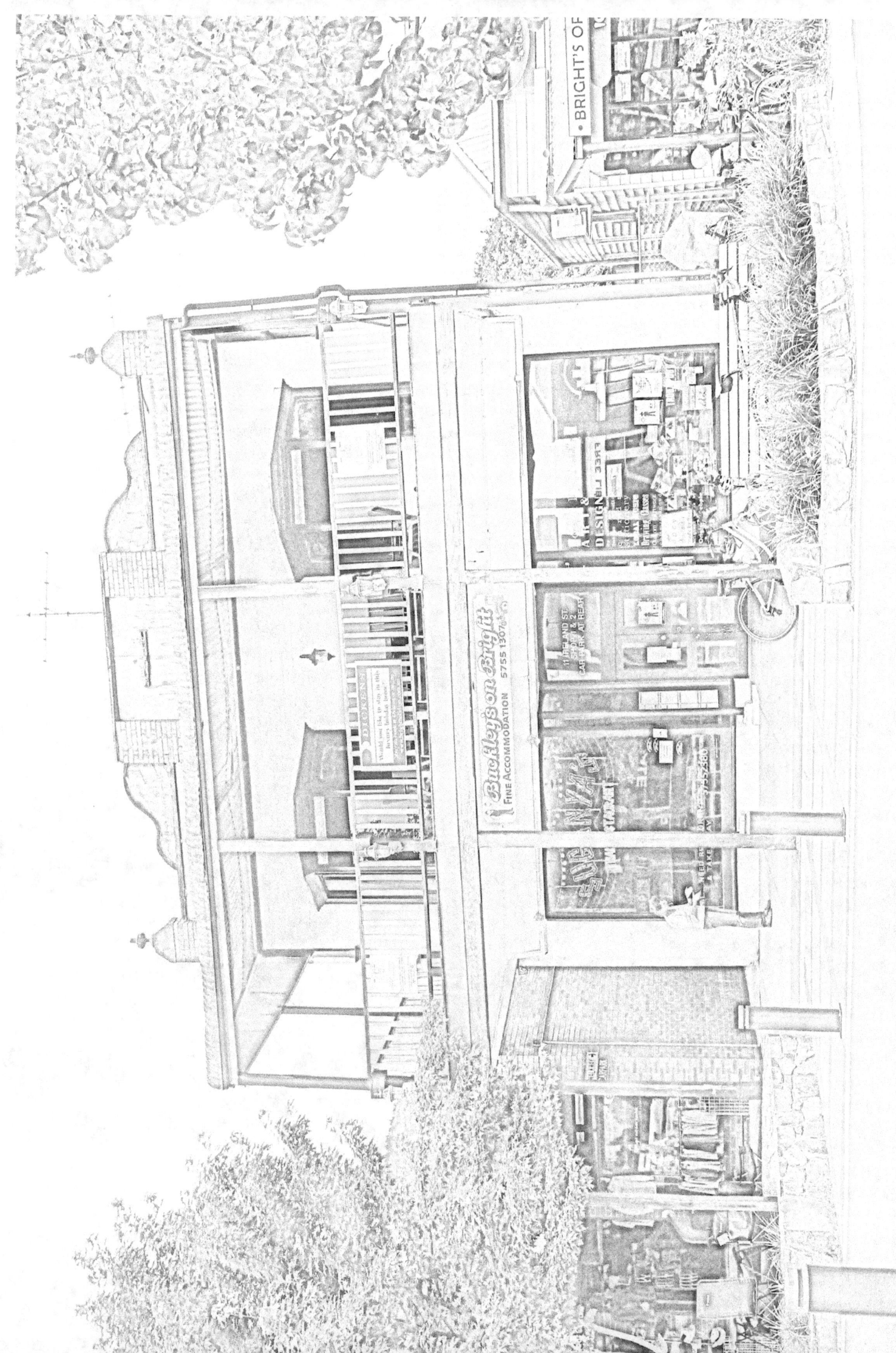

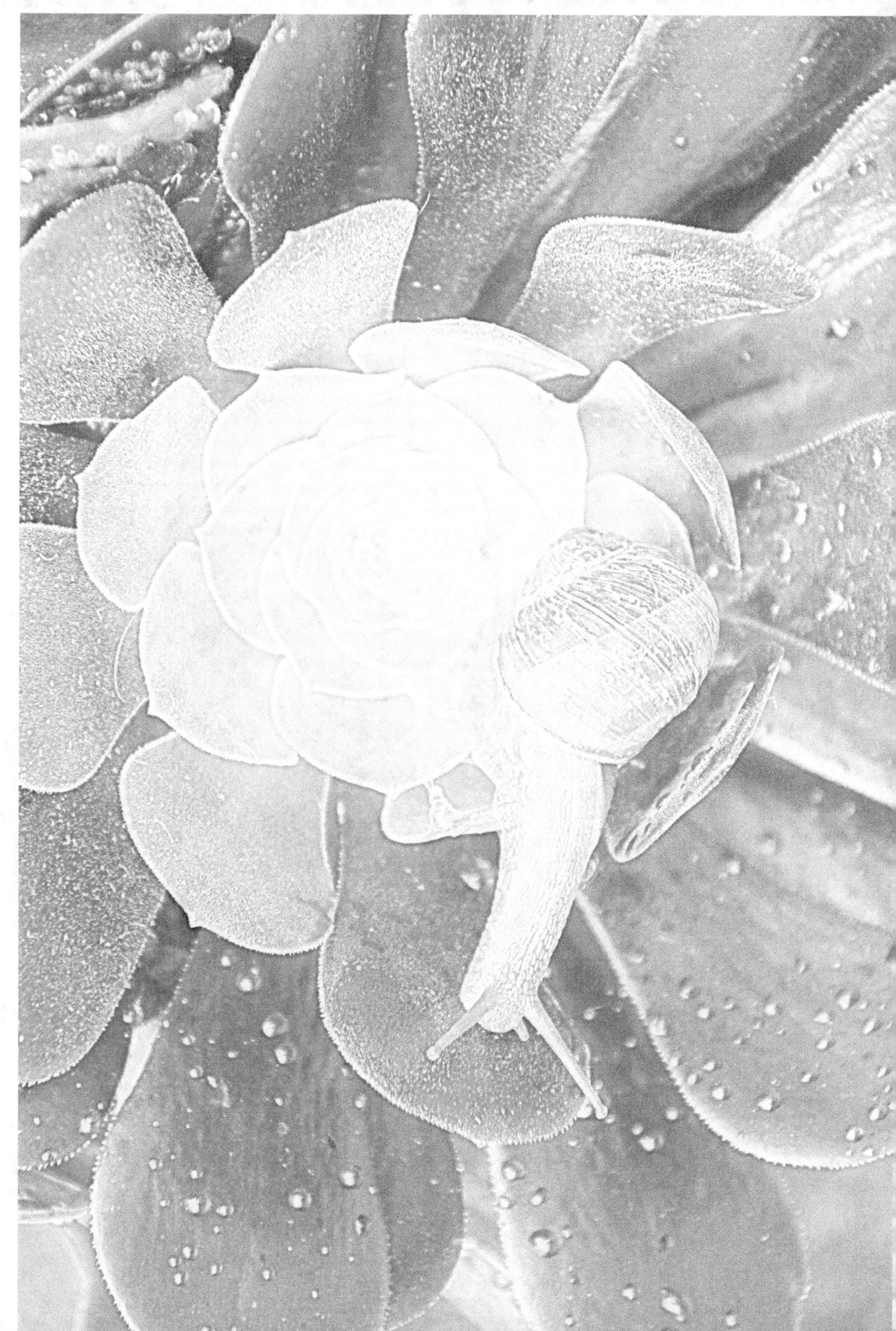

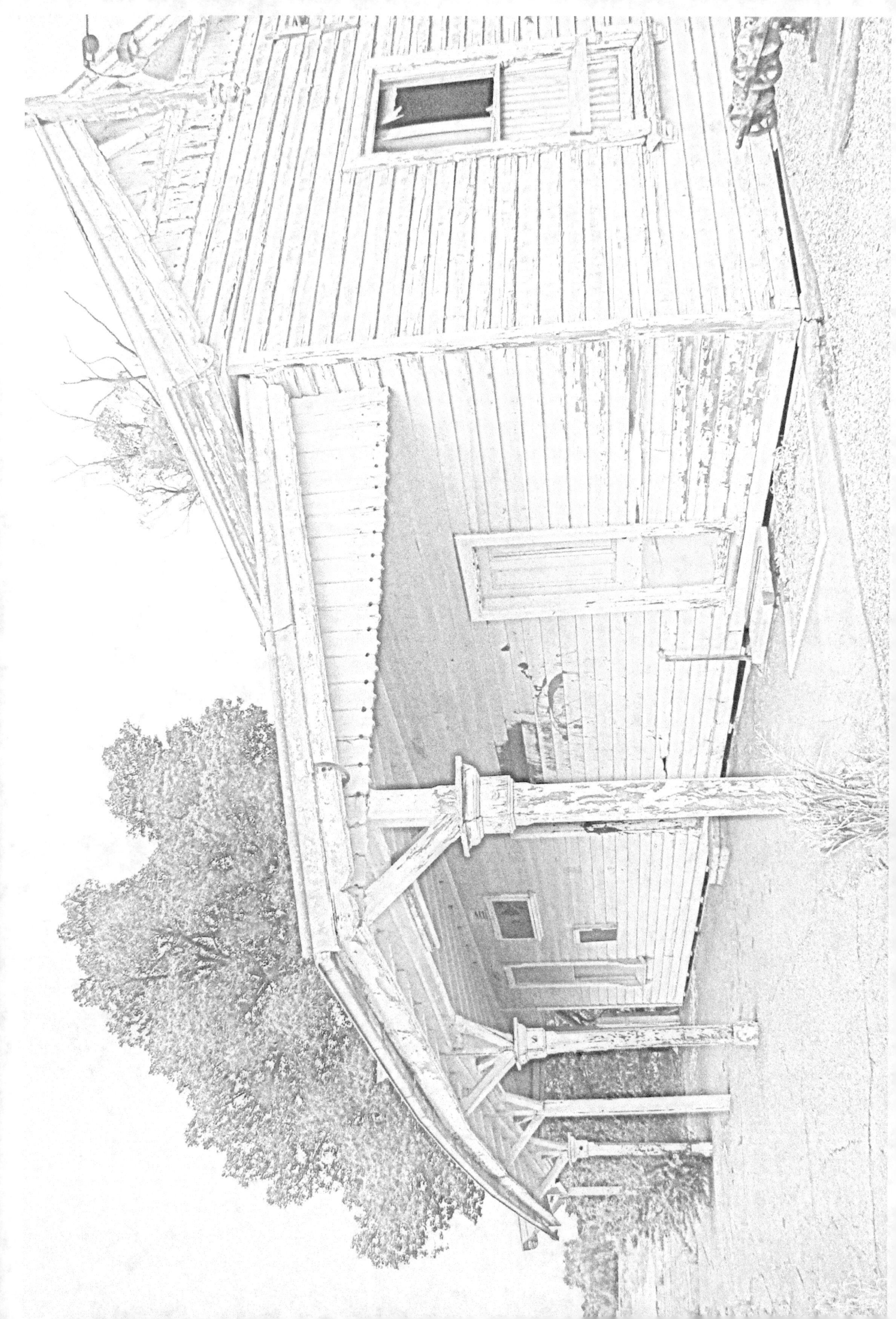

Surf Rescue

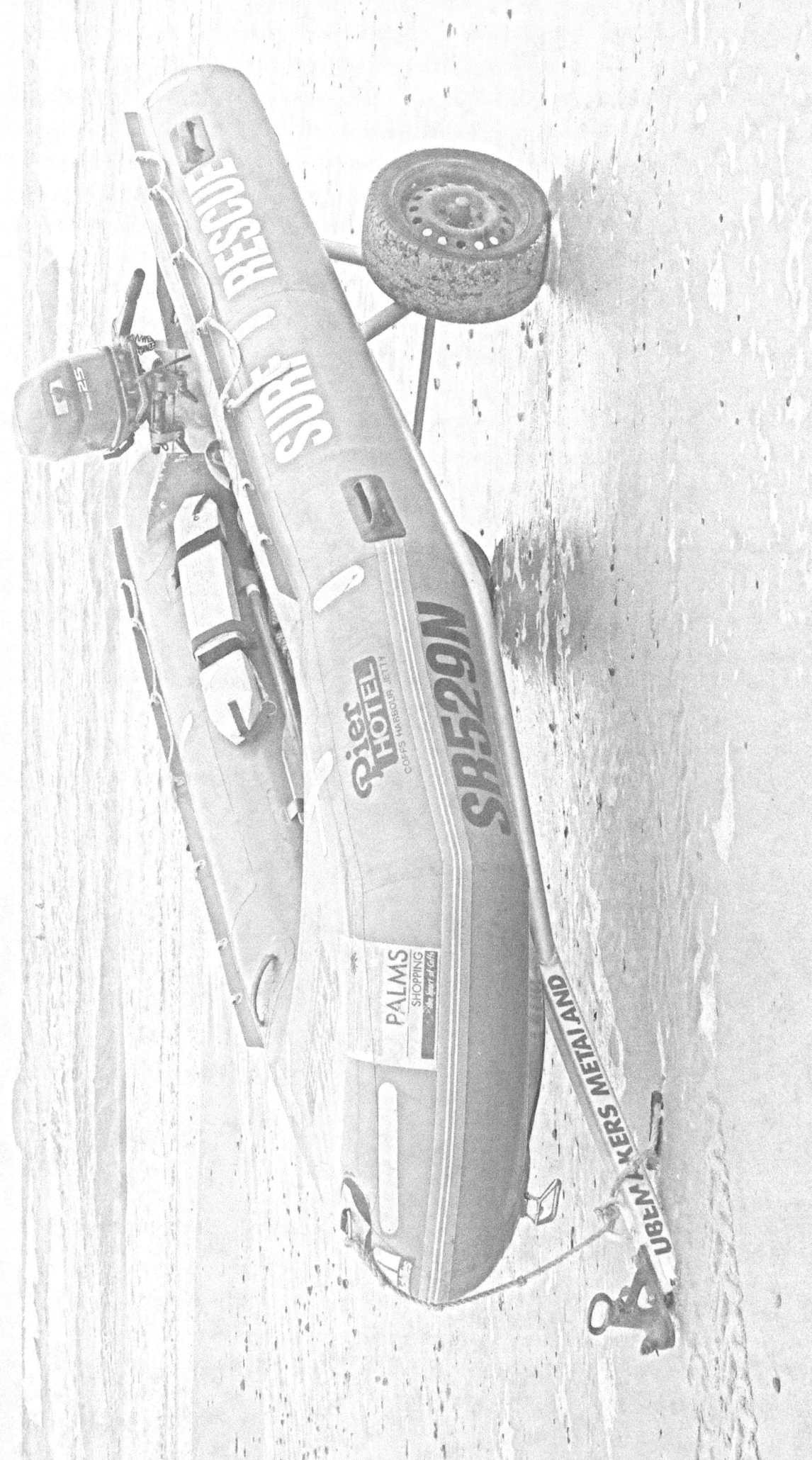

Steam Train

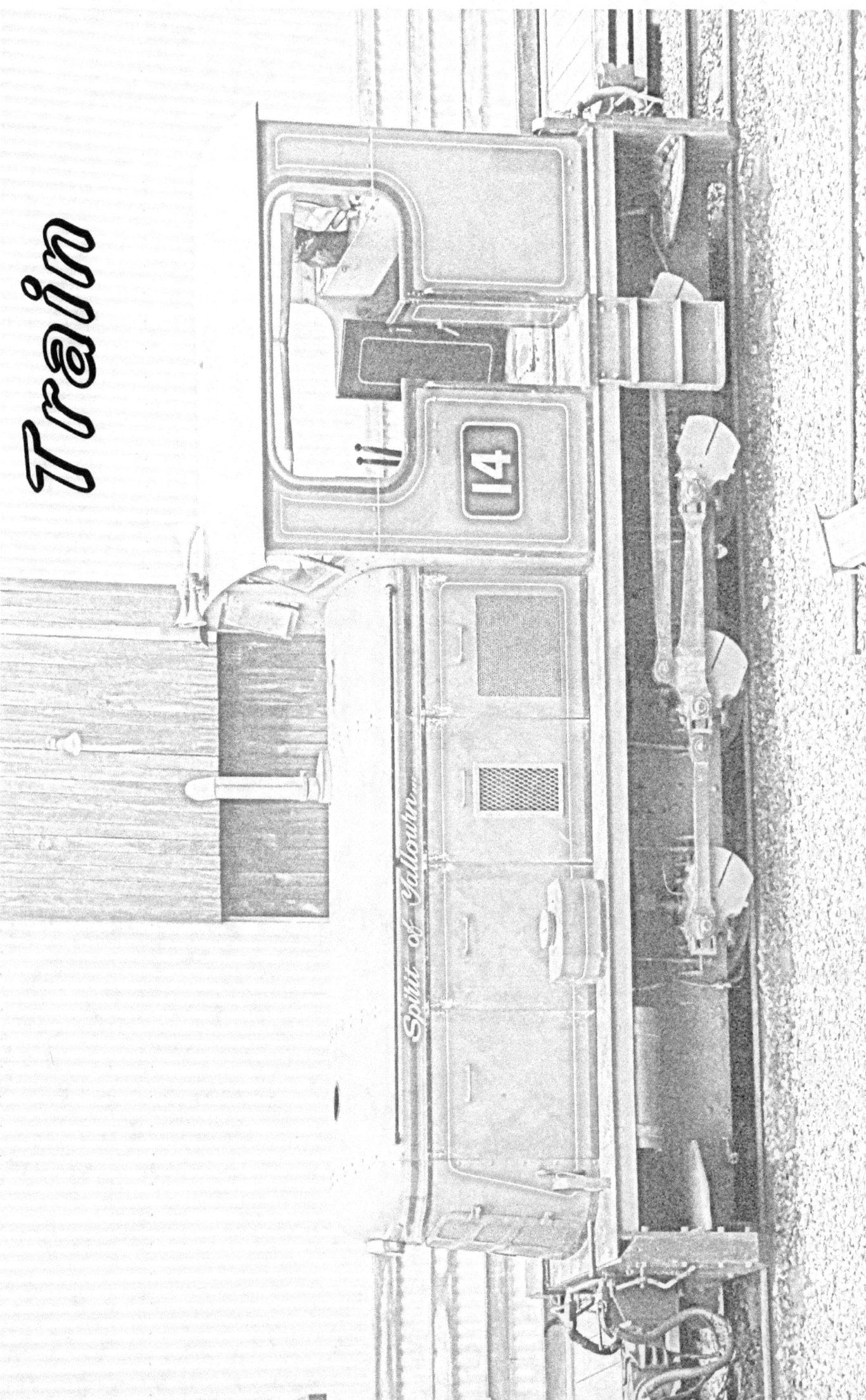

Train

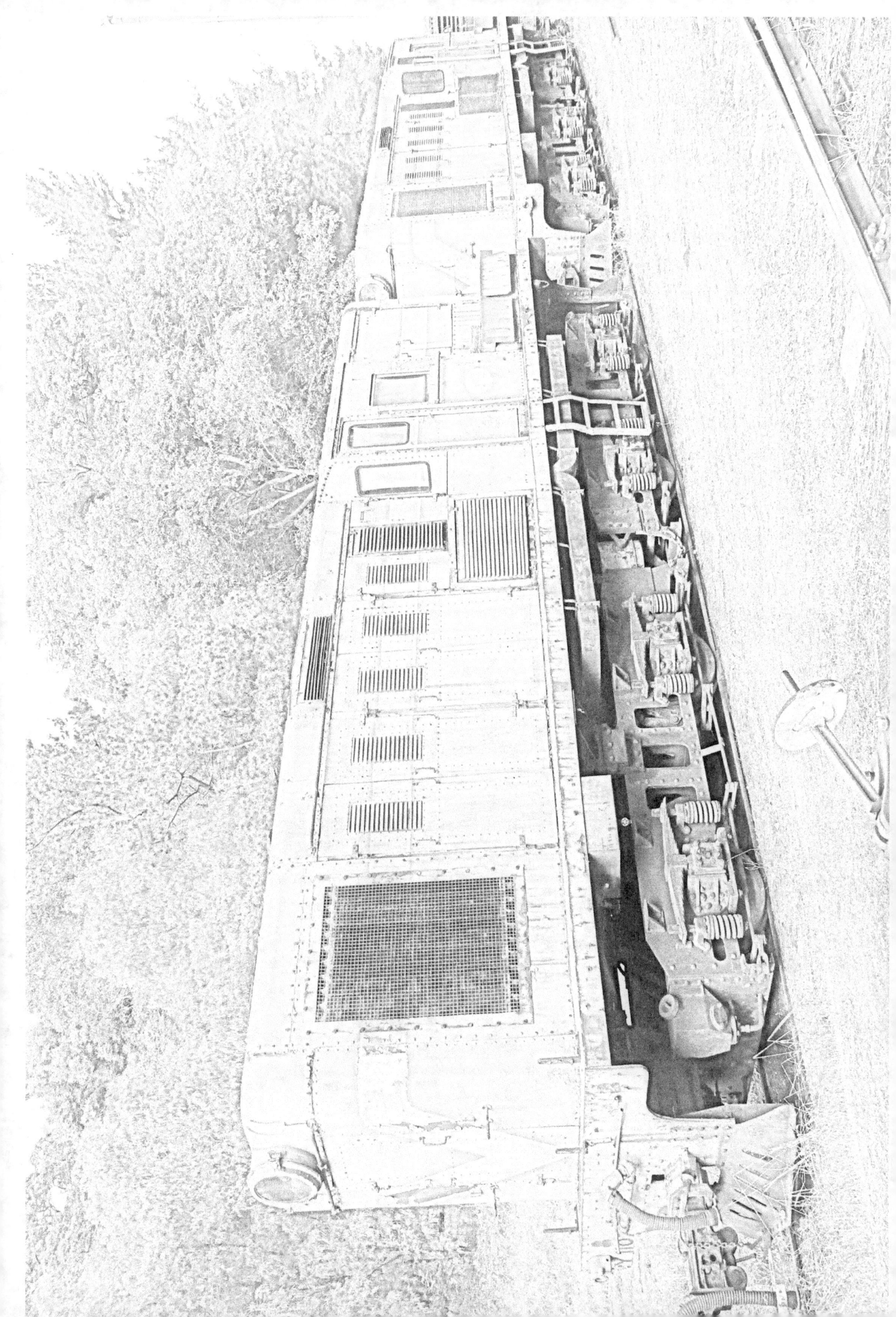

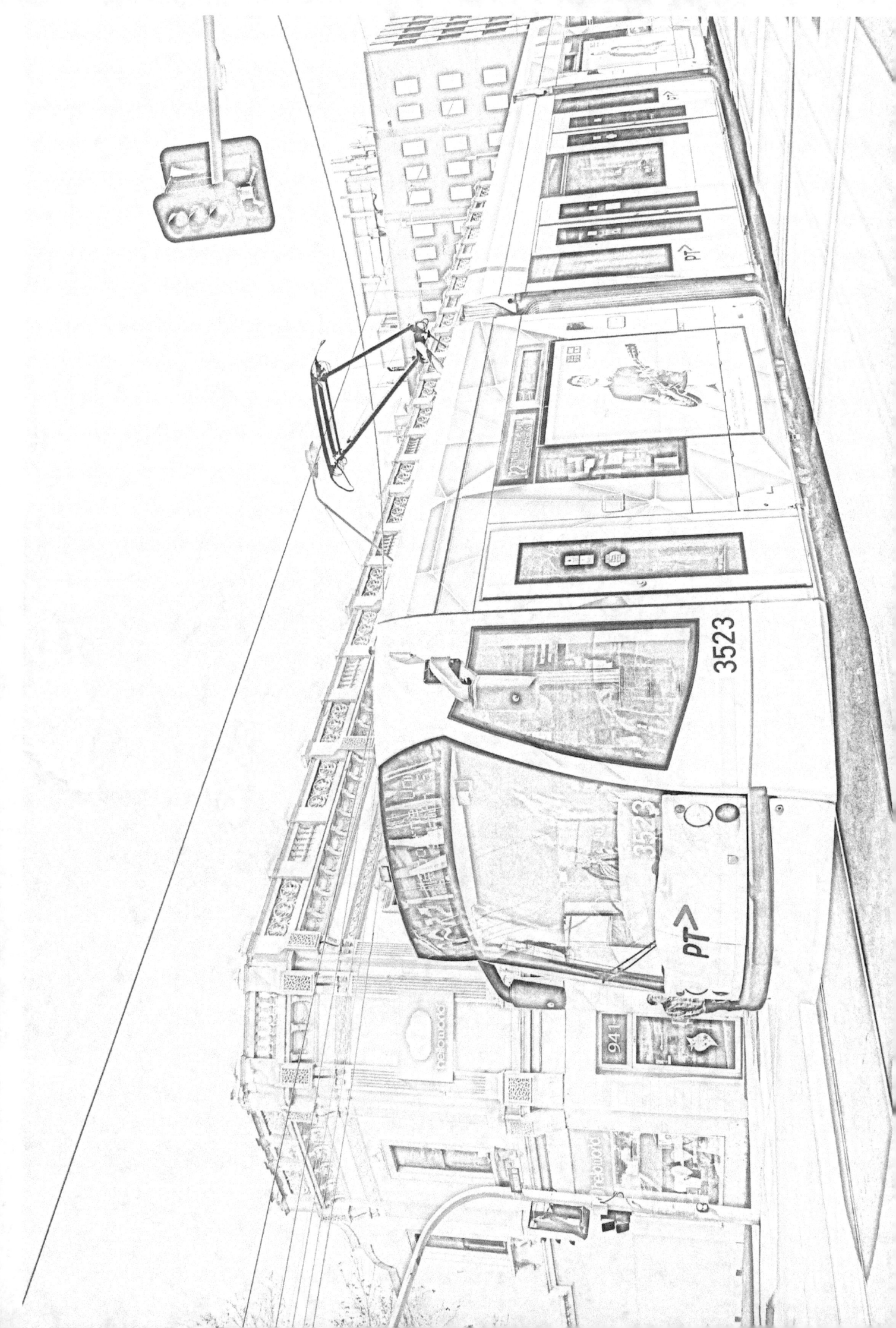

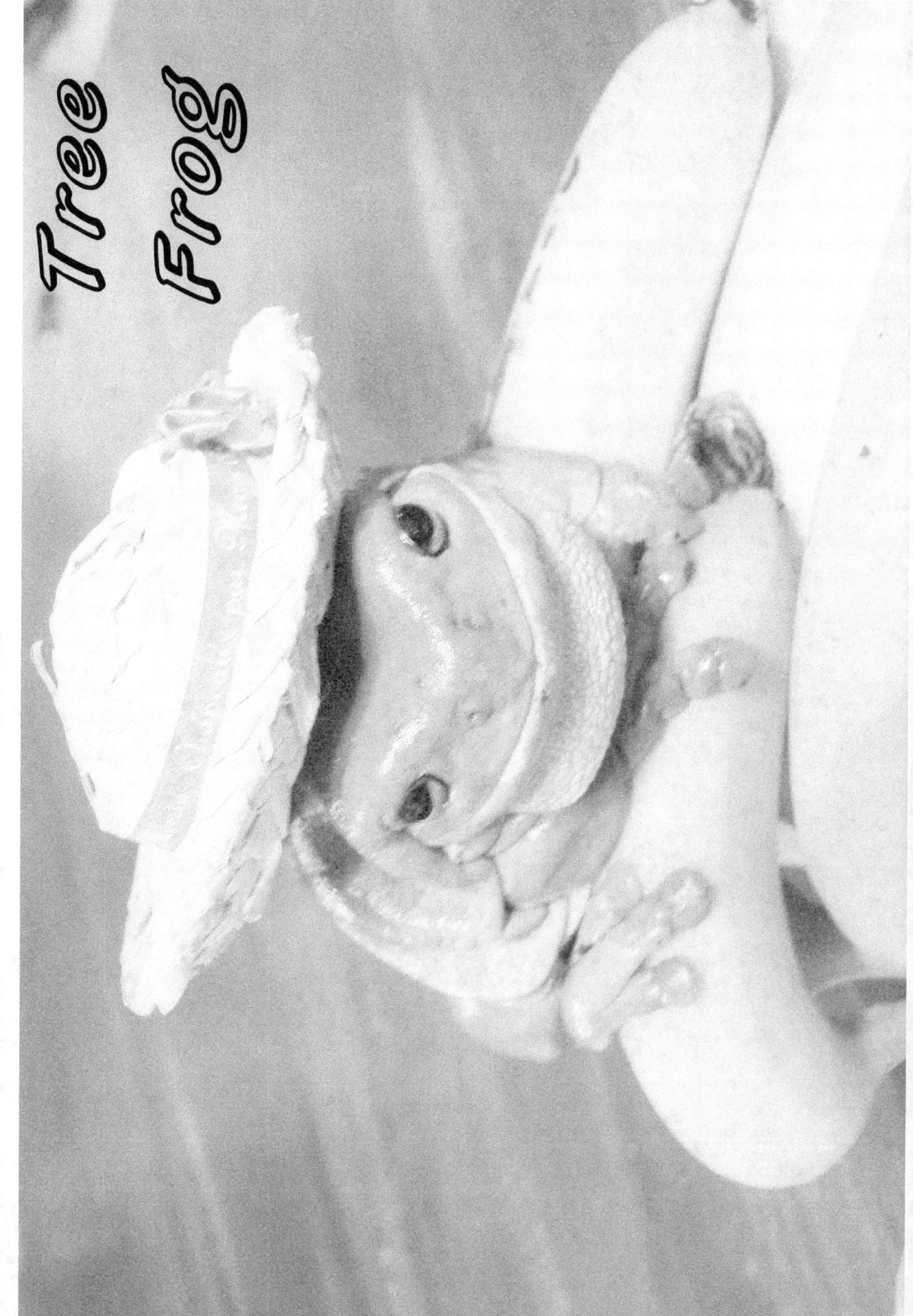

Tree Frog

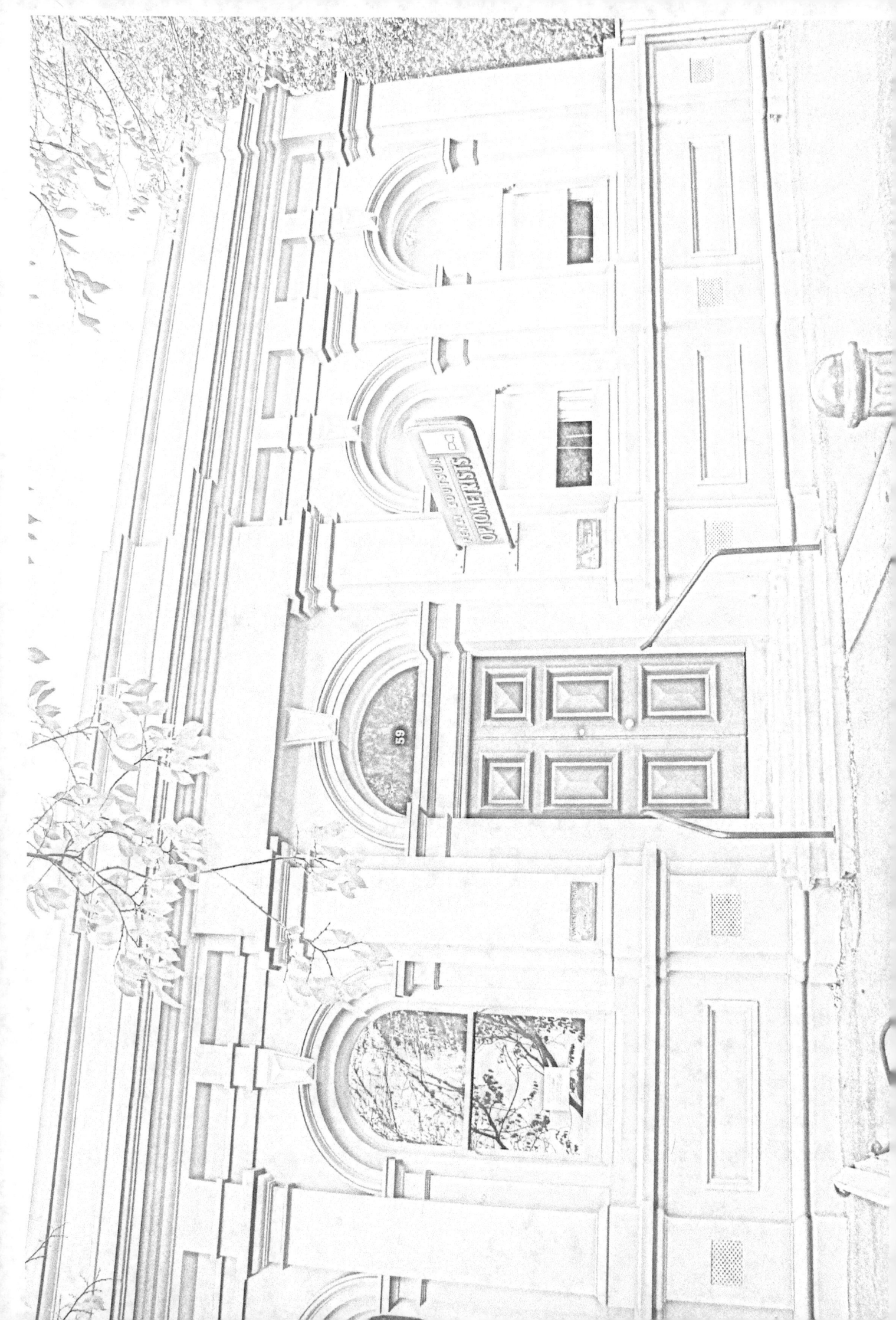

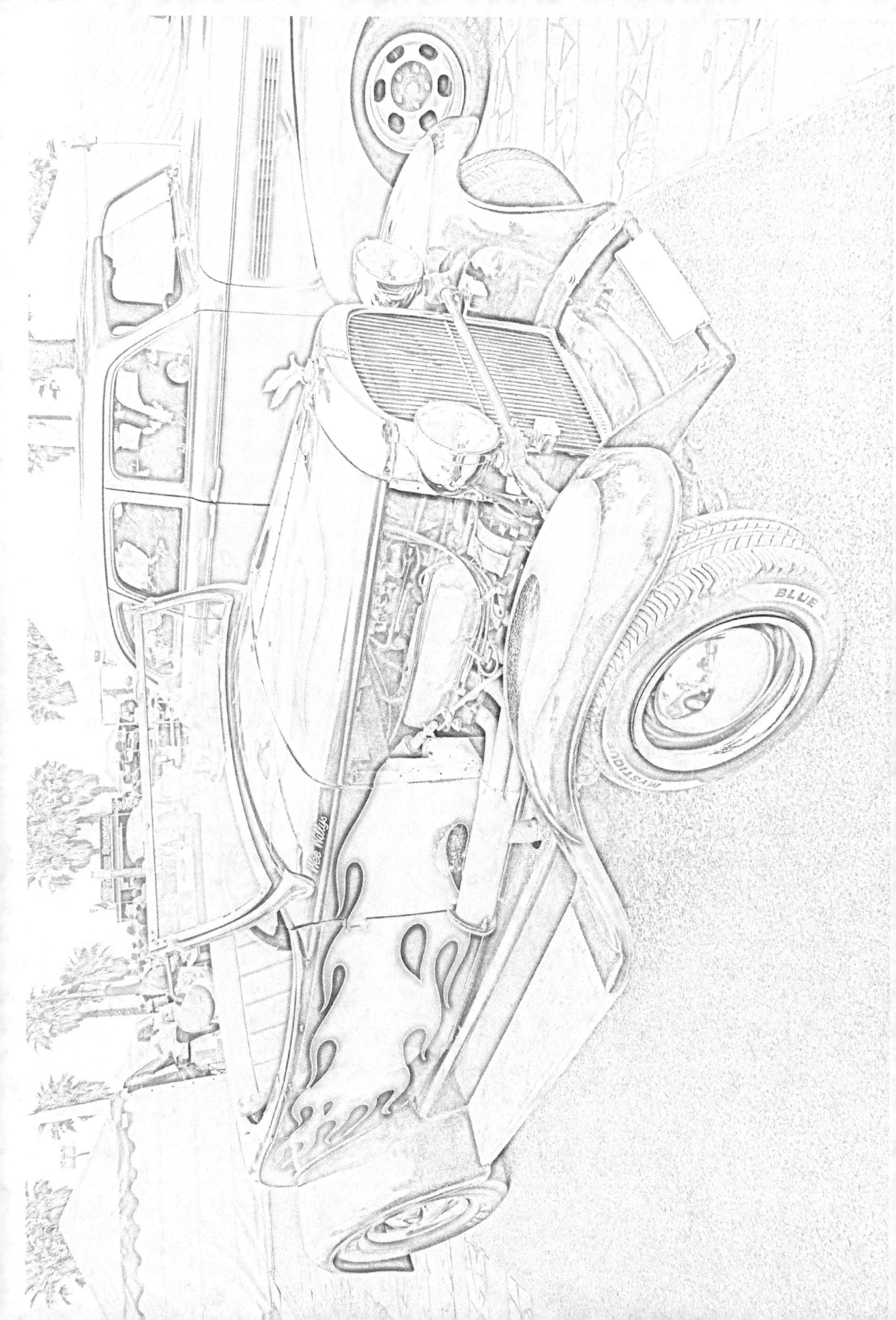

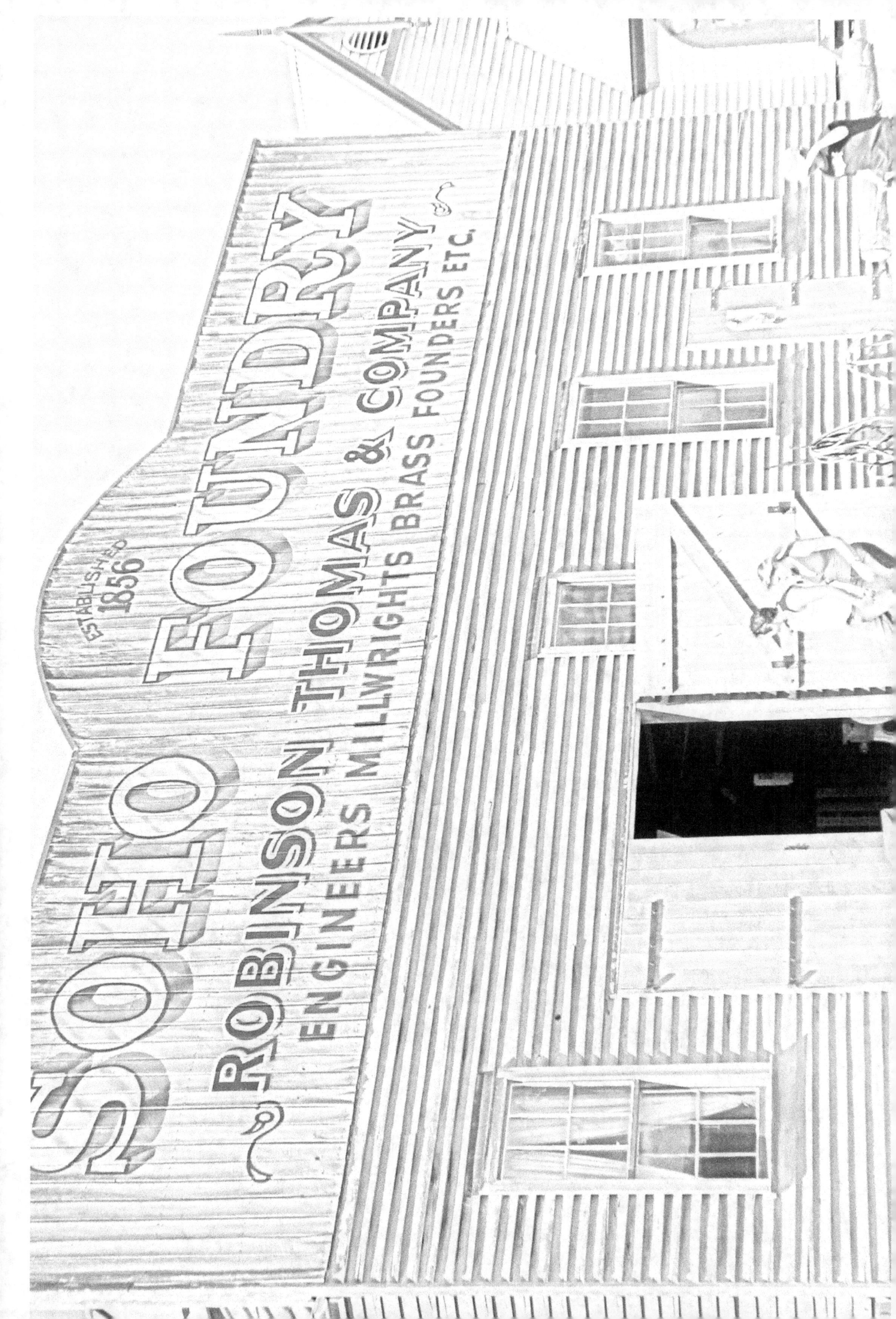

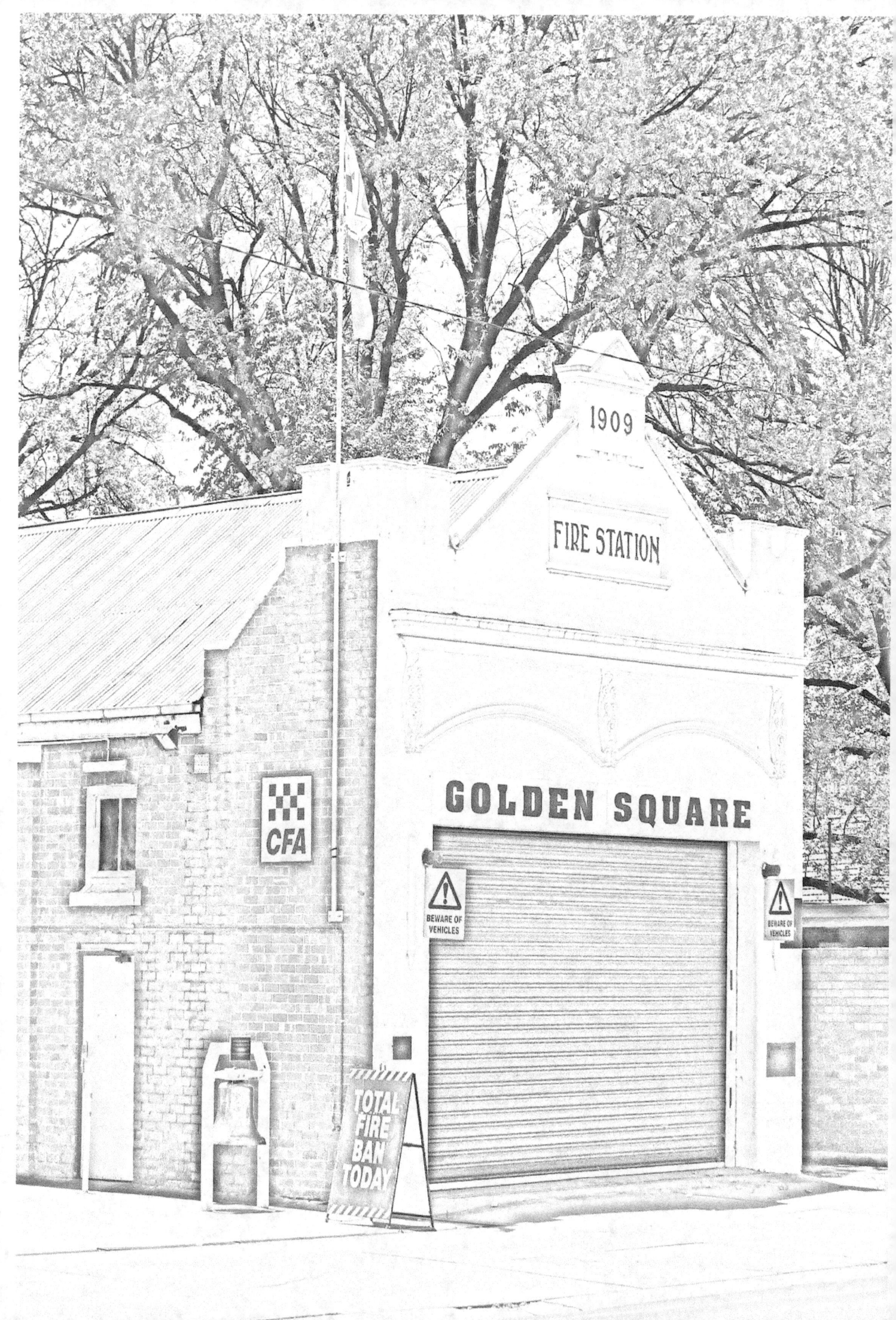

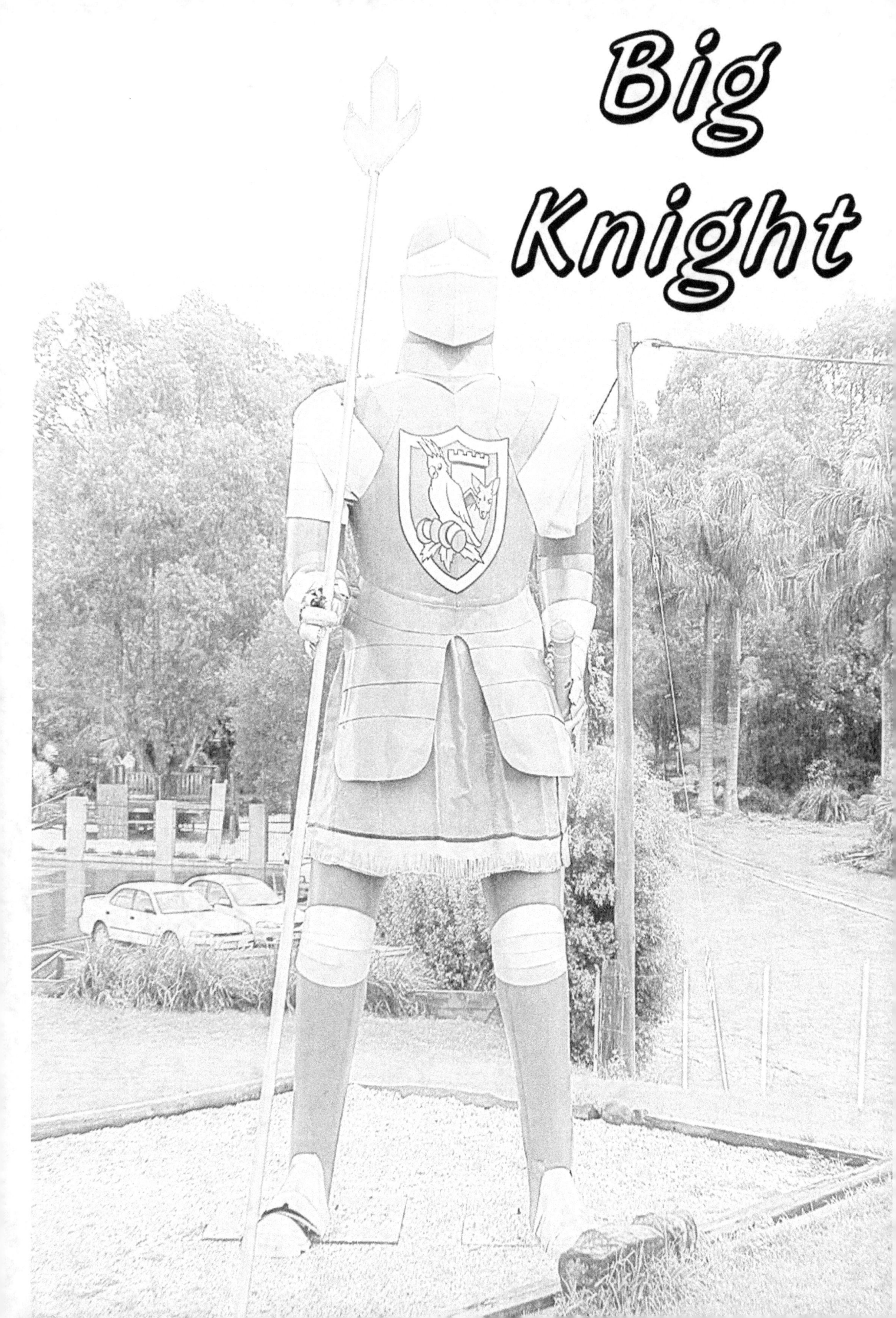

Big Knight

Cormorant

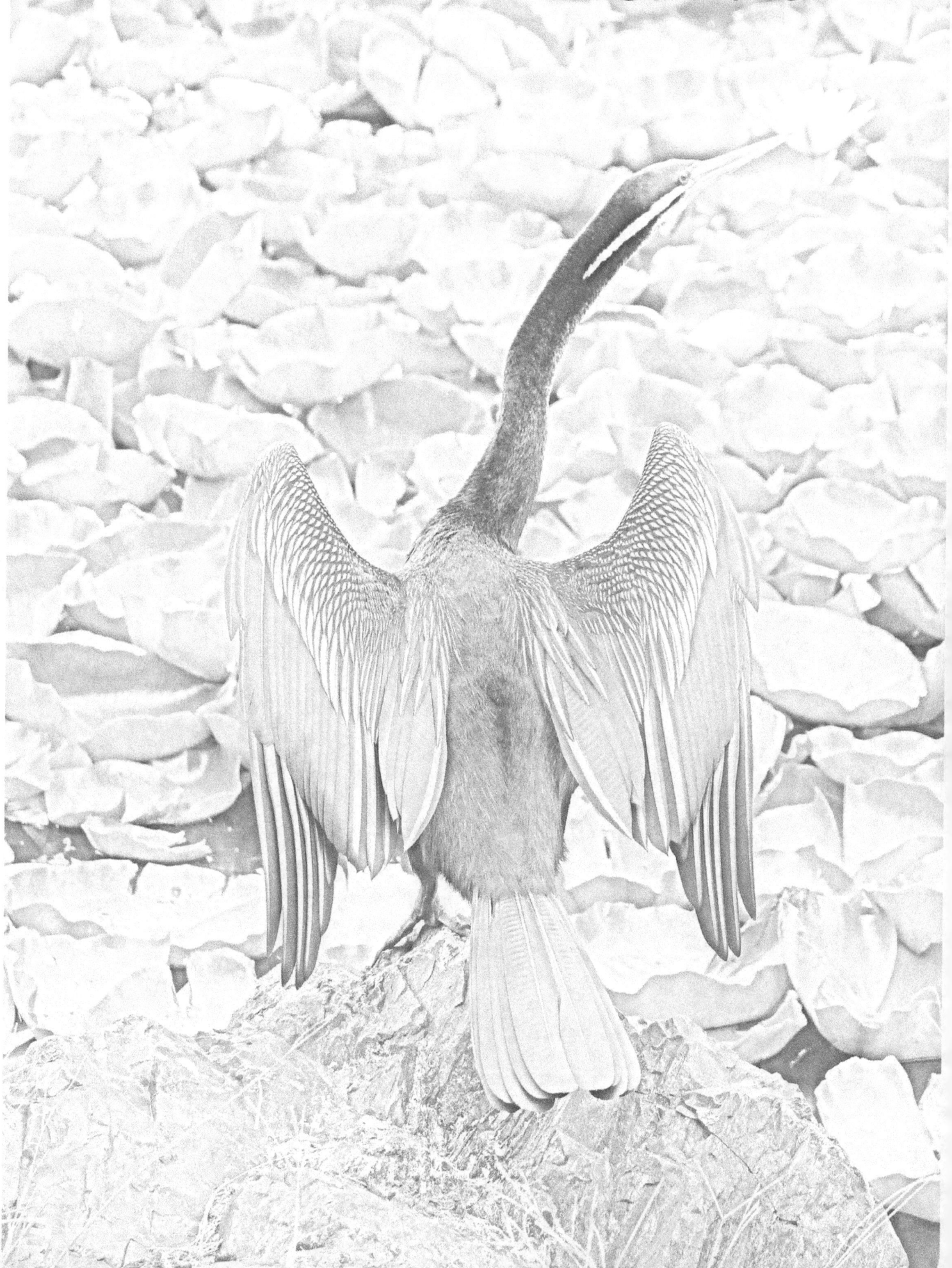

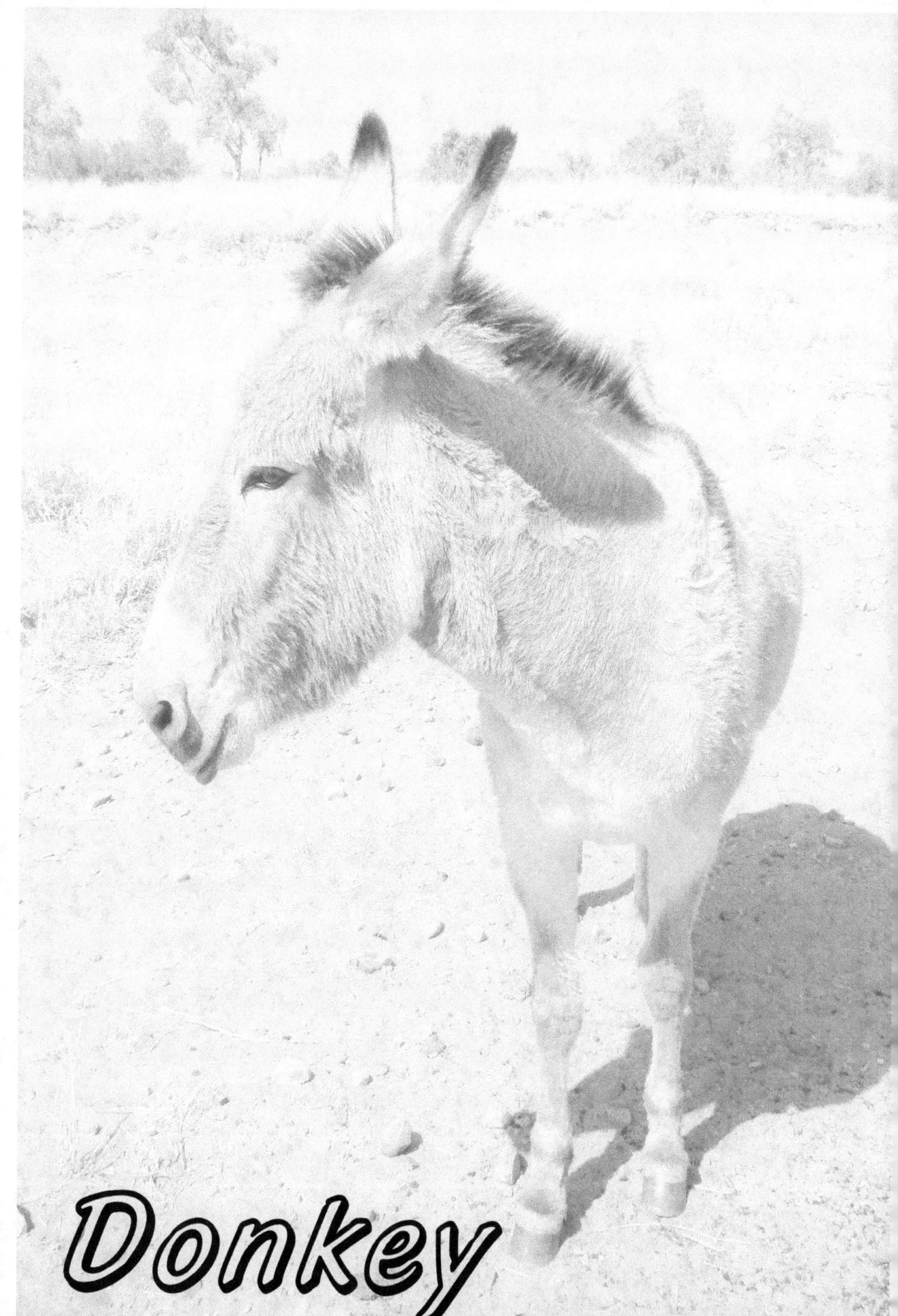

Donkey

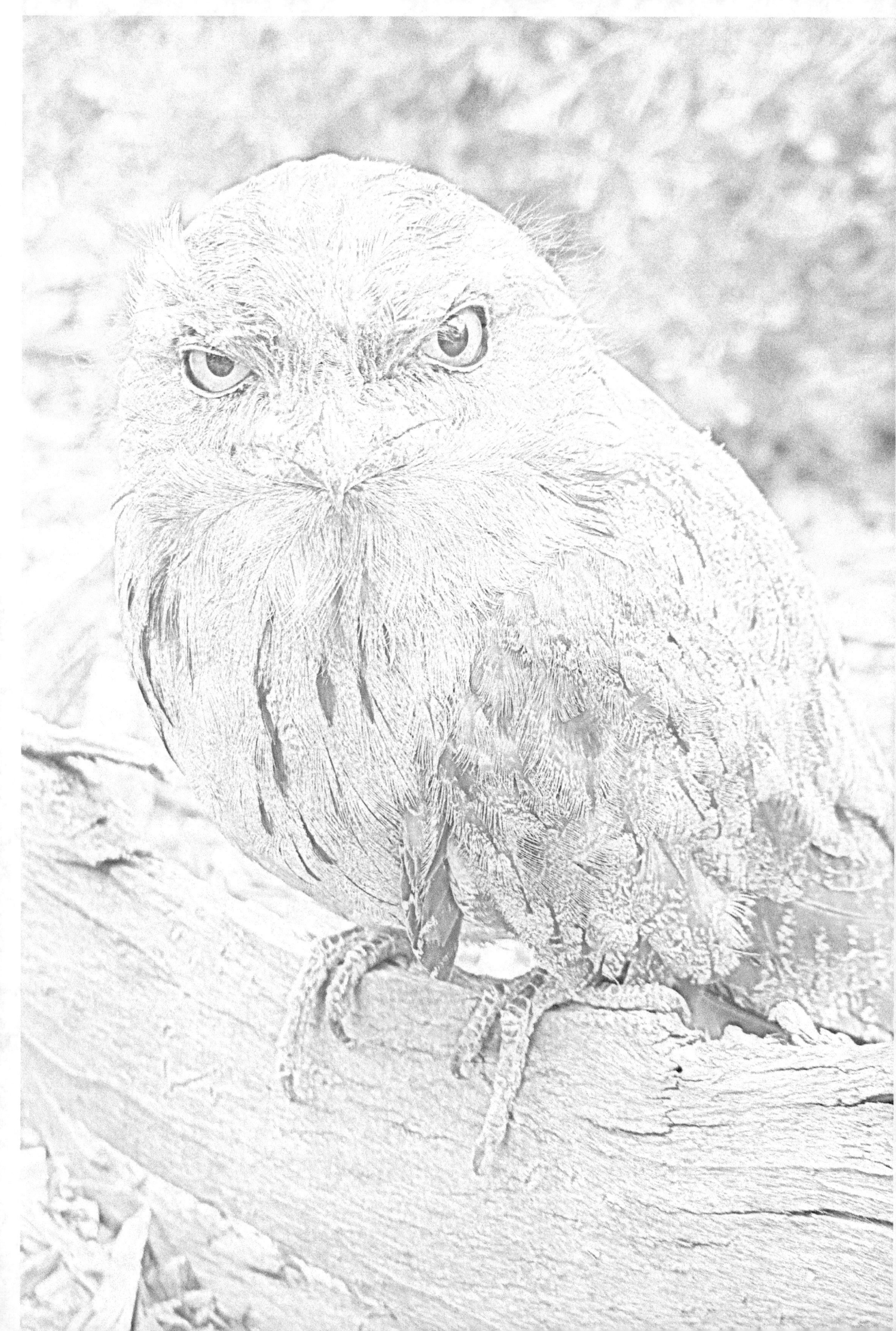

Lighthouse

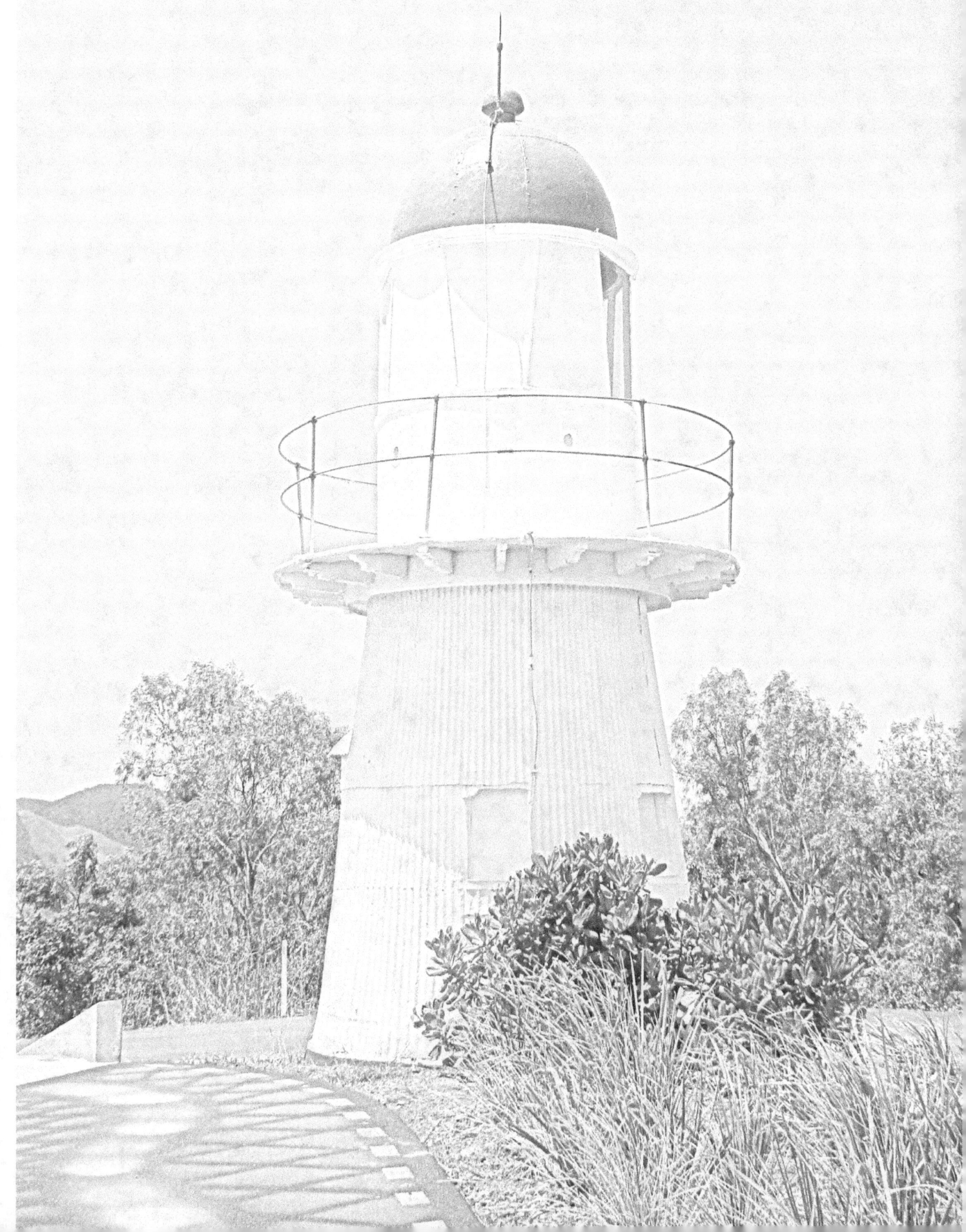

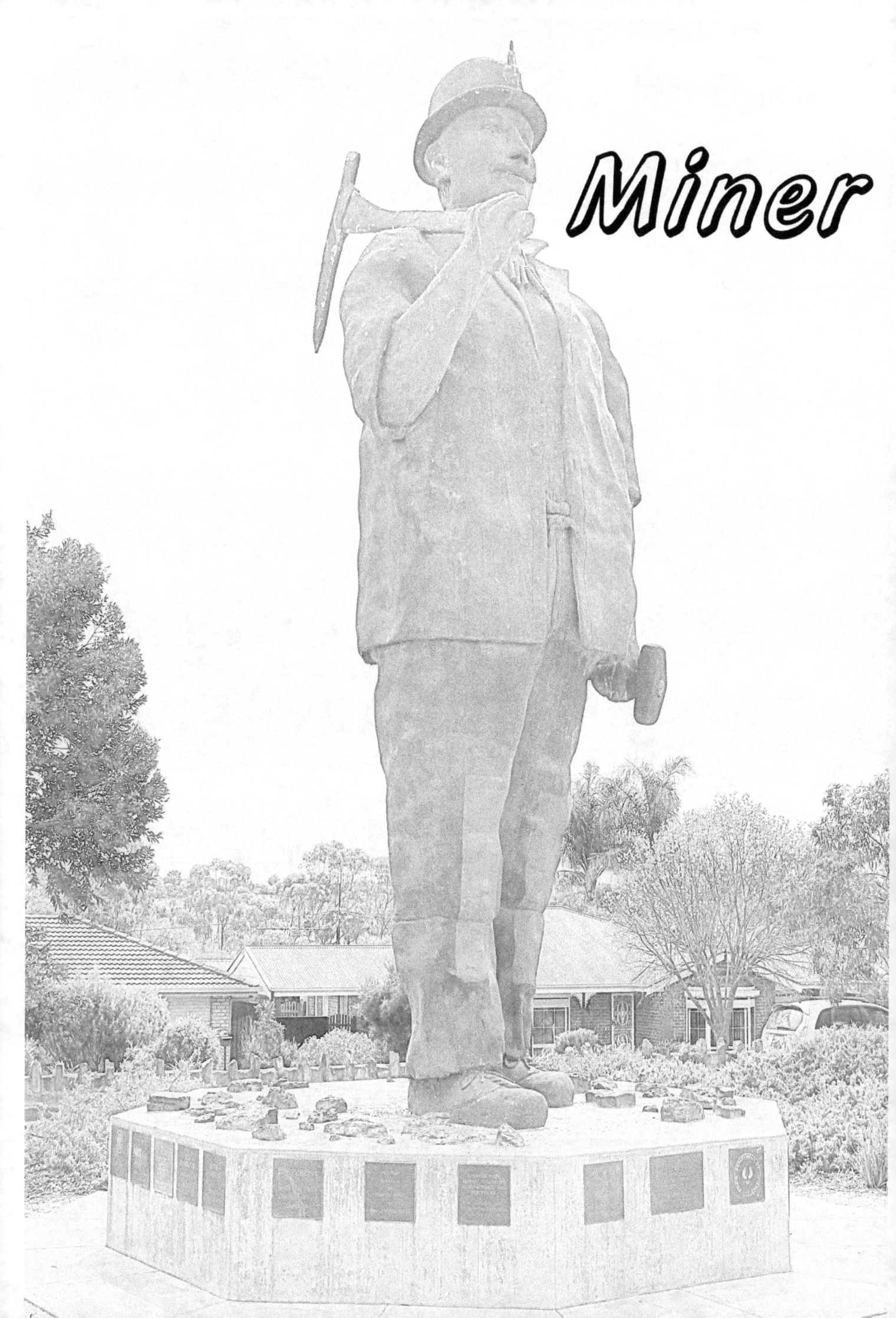

Miner

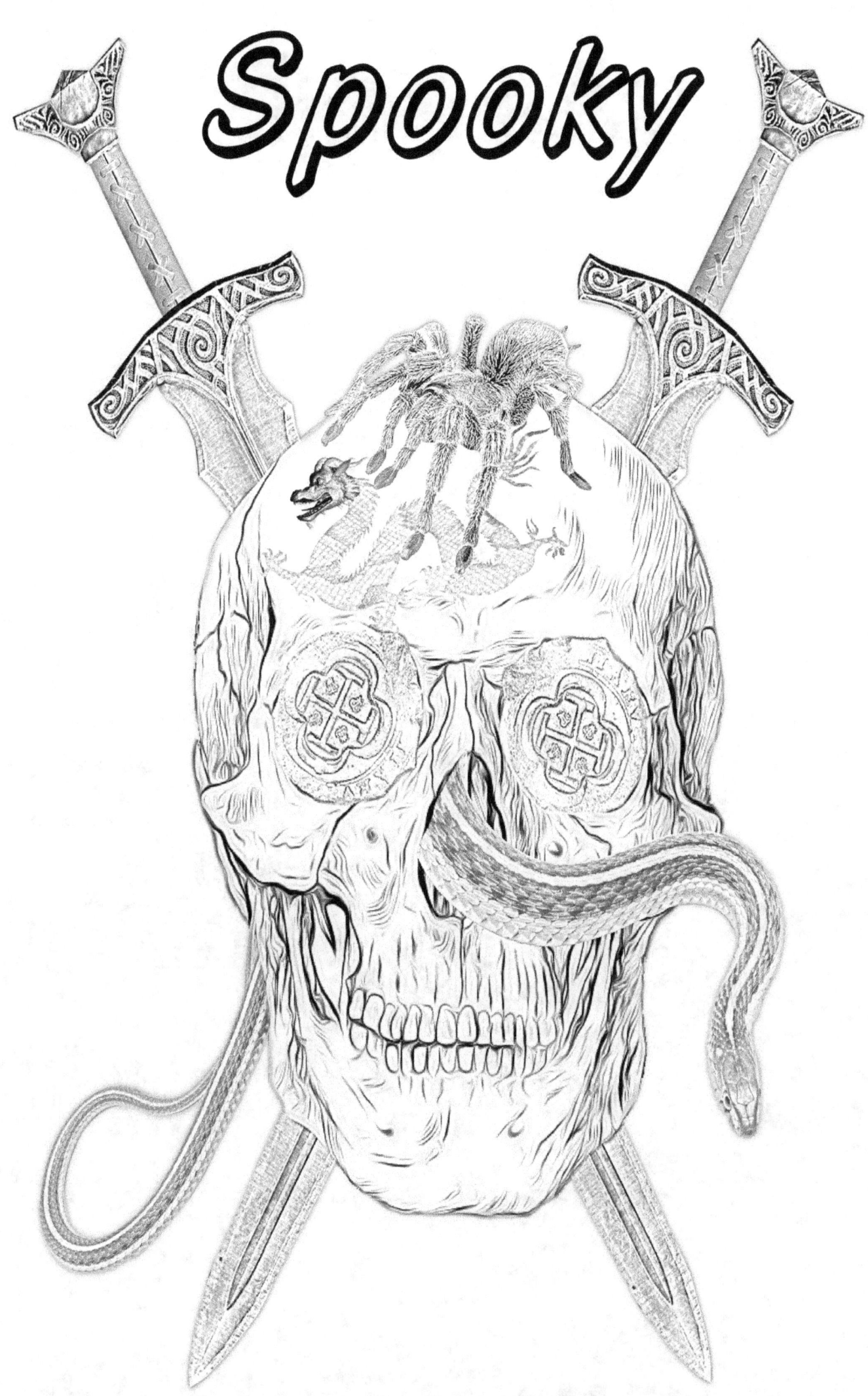

Windmill

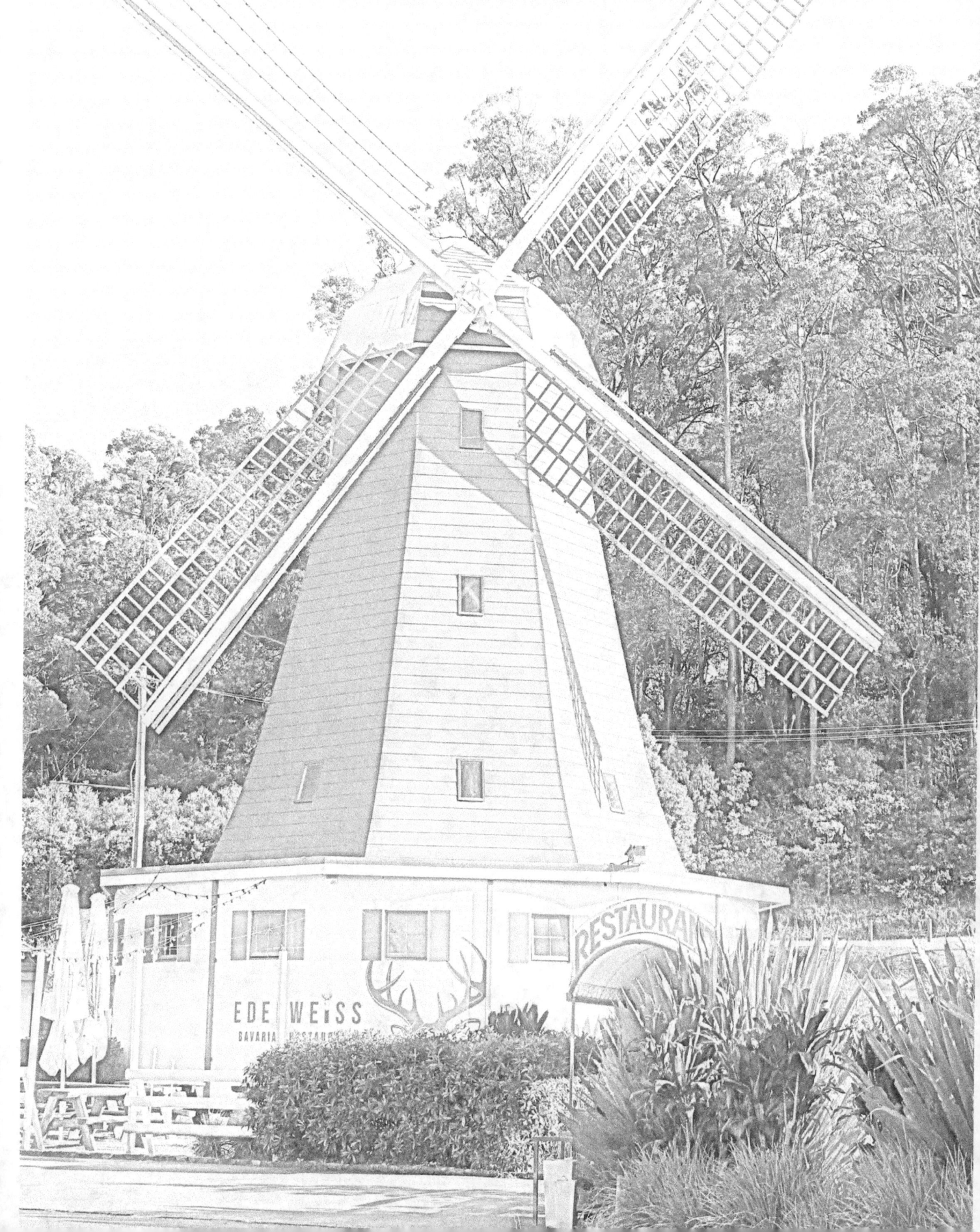